The Practitioner Inquiry Series

Marilyn Cochran-Smith and Susan L. Lytle, *SERIES EDITORS*

Teaching Mathematics to the New Standards: Relearning the Dance
RUTH M. HEATON

Action, Talk, and Text: Learning and Teaching Through Inquiry
GORDON WELLS, Editor

Teacher Narrative as Citical Inquiry: Rewriting the Script
JOY S. RITCHIE & DAVID E. WILSON

From Another Angle: Children s Strengths and School Standards
MARGARET HIMLEY with PATRICIA F. CARINI, E ditors

Unplayed Tapes: A Personal History of Collaborative Teacher Research
STEPHEN M. FISHMAN & LUCILLE McCARTHY

Inside City Schools: Investigating Literacy in the Multicultural Classroom
SARAH WARSHAUER FREEDMAN, ELIZABETH RADIN SIMONS, JULIE SHALHOPE KALNIN, ALEX CASARENO, and the M-CLASS TEAMS

Class Actions: Teaching for Social Justice in Elementary and Middle School
JoBETH ALLEN, Editor

Teacher/Mentor: A Dialogue for Collaborative Learning
PEG GRAHAM, SALLY HUDSON-ROSS, CHANDRA ADKINS, PATTI M cWHORTER, & JENNIFER McDUFFIE STEWART, E ditors

Teaching Other People s Children: Literacy and Learning in a Bilingual Classroom
CYNTHIA BALLENGER

Teaching, Multimedia, and Mathematics: Investigations of Real Practice
MAGDALENE LAMPERT & DEBORAH LOEWENBERG BALL

Tensions of Teaching: Beyond Tips to Critical Reflection
JUDITH M. NEWMAN

John Dewey and the Challenge of Classroom Practice
STEPHEN M. FISHMAN & LUCILLE McCARTHY

Sometimes I Can Be Anything : Power, Gender, and Identity in a Primary Classroom
KAREN GALLAS

Learning in Small Moments: Life in an Urban Classroom
DANIEL R. MEIER

Interpreting Teacher Practice: Two Continuing Stories
RENATE SCHULZ

Creating Democratic Classrooms: The Struggle to Integrate Theory and Practice
LANDON E. BEYER, Editor

Teaching Mathematics to the New Standards

RELEARNING THE DANCE

RUTH M. HEATON

Foreword by Magdalene Lampert

TEACHERS COLLEGE PRESS

Teachers College, Columbia University
New York and London

This work is sponsored in part by the Center for the Learning and Teaching of Elementary Subjects, Institute for Research on Teaching, Michigan State University. The Center for the Learning and Teaching of Elementary Subjects is funded primarily by the Office of Educational Research and Improvement, U.S. Department of Education. The opinions expressed in this publication do not necessarily reflect the position, policy, or endorsement of the Office or the Department (Cooperative Agreement No. G0087C0226).

Published by Teachers College Press, 1234 Amsterdam Avenue, New York, NY 10027

Library of Congress Cataloging-in-Publication Data

Heaton, Ruth M.
Teaching mathematics to the new standards : relearning the dance / Ruth M. Heaton; foreword by Magdalene Lampert.
p. cm. — (Practitioner inquiry series)
Includes bibliographical references and index.
ISBN 0-8077-3969-3 (cloth : alk. paper) — ISBN 0-8077-3968-5 (pbk. : alk. paper)
1. Mathematics—Study and teaching—United States. I. Title. II. Series.
QA13 .H43 2000
510.71'073—dc21 00-030237

ISBN 0-8077-3968-5 (paper)
ISBN 0-8077-3969-3 (cloth)

Printed on acid-free paper
Manufactured in the United States of America

07 06 05 04 03 02 01 00 8 7 6 5 4 3 2 1

To Steve

Contents

Foreword

"Teachers as learners" and the newer "learning in and from practice" are popular phrases in the education world. It is easy enough to endorse these ideas, but we have very few portraits of what these words actually might mean, either to the teacher in question or in terms of the instructional activities in which the teacher is engaged. Ruth Heaton has written an account of her attempts to change the way she teaches elementary mathematics that not only describes that learning process but gives us insight into what supports it and what gets in the way. She learns a new way to teach *while teaching*, but she also learns that this new way of teaching involves her in a never-ending process of investigation. In the chapters that follow, she paints a detailed picture of how and why learning in and from practice is a fundamental element of the kind of teaching she is trying to do.

Another pair of slogans that appear often in conversations about teaching are "teachers need to know both their subject and their students," and "they need to be able to integrate these two kinds of knowledge in making instructional decisions." Heaton learns mathematics as she teaches, not only at the level that she wants her students to know it, but at a level that enables her to appreciate why the curriculum is designed the way it is. She also adds considerably to her knowledge of how fourth graders think about mathematics and how they act in the face of mathematical challenges. In her portrayal of her work, we see the constant interplay of teacher, students, and subject matter that David Hawkins (1974) has made us aware of. This tripartite relationship comes through on nearly every page that Heaton has written.

We have long understood that it is not possible to bypass teachers in delivering powerful subject matter to students. Here we see what is entailed for the teacher in mediating between that subject matter and learners in classrooms. Heaton gets us started on the work that needs to be done to help teachers acquire the subject matter knowledge that they obviously need, and to acquire it in ways that will be usable in practice. By sticking closely to a text, Heaton demonstrates how a teacher can study mathematics by working at the intersection of good curriculum materials and student responses to those materials (Cohen & Hill, 1997). But the most interesting thing we learn from her efforts is that such study is necessary. She demonstrates in vivid detail what the problems are with imagining that instruction can be substantially improved by creating "teacher proof curriculum."

Although we often hear that we have learned as a profession not to rely on simple mechanisms like texts and tests to bring about instructional change, we go on pouring money into creating new and better curricula and new and better assessments, without recognizing the teacher learning agenda that such materials demand. In mathematics education in particular, serious efforts have gone into creating higher standards for curriculum, instruction, and assessment to respond to expanded intellectual demands in the workplace and newly available technologies. Many new textbook series have been published that are congruent with these standards, and assessments have been designed to reflect the changes. But we have yet to invest substantially in the teacher development that it will take to make use of these texts and assessments. Heaton shows us how learning mathematics in the context of practice is different from both learning mathematics in college courses and learning methods of teaching mathematics. We are only beginning to generate ideas about how to restructure preservice and inservice education of teachers so that it can include the investigation of mathematical ideas in relation to the teaching and learning of those ideas (Darling-Hammond, 1997; Lampert & Ball, 1998).

Looking at Heaton's teaching from an entirely different angle, we see what is implied in saying that teachers cannot succeed without having their students succeed because teachers depend on their students to produce the outcomes of their work (Cohen, 1988). Research has found that many teachers cope with this dependence by expecting less of their students (Lortie, 1975; Powell, Farrar, & Cohen, 1985; Sedlak, Wheeler, Pullin, & Cusick, 1986). As we read Heaton's description of her attempts to teach serious mathematics to fourth graders, we see many points where it seems as if she could make her job easier by expecting less of them. After all, they *do* participate actively in problem-solving activities, and they *do* engage in discussions with their classmates—two indications of learning that do not appear consistently in American classrooms (Schmidt, 1996). That they also should be deeply engaged with learning important mathematics may be just too much to hope for. As she learns what it means for students to be engaged with important mathematics, Heaton does not lower her expectations, and she is bold in sharing the struggles that result.

Reading Heaton's story, it is tempting to say, "Yes, but . . . " Yes, but she had a lot of support. Yes, but she was surrounded by people who think deeply about teaching and learning and mathematics. Yes, but she taught in a special kind of school. So what can we learn from her story about the change process of more "ordinary teachers"? It seems to me we can learn many things, but here I will mention two. We can learn about the practice that teachers will need to change *toward* if curriculum and instruction are to be improved in the ways that new standards suggest. For example, we see that opening up classroom discourse to take students' ideas seriously requires a kind of knowledge that cannot simply be acquired and then applied. It requires both preparation and the capacity to invent practice in the moment. The second point that relates Heaton's story to the work of more "ordinary" teachers is drawn from recent research on professional development and teacher communities. In a variety of settings, it seems clear that higher teacher expectations for student learning and the concurrent use of new practices to teach them are most likely to be found in settings where teachers *have* a professional community and make regular and consistent use of external supports for their work (Elmore, Peterson, & McCarthey, 1996; McLaughlin, Talbert, & Bascia, 1990). Rather than seeing Heaton's situation as extraordinary, we might need to invest considerable resources in making situations like hers more typical in order to produce a higher level of student achievement.

Finally, we can learn something from Heaton's work about the interplay between the personal and the professional in teacher growth. Because she has been willing to share her struggles in a way that is academically rigorous and related to many important educational questions, we have much more here than a poignant autobiography. But we do have enough of an autobiography to understand that teacher change means a fundamental change in one's personal identity, not just learning new skills or acquiring new knowledge. That Heaton has been able to tell her story in a way that is not overly sentimental or romantic makes it both compelling reading and useful to teacher educators and scholars.

Magdalene Lampert
University of Michigan

Acknowledgments

I am deeply appreciative of the classroom teacher who graciously shared her time and insights and the fourth-grade students who became instrumental in my learning. I am thankful for what I learned from colleagues on the Mathematics and Teaching through Hypermedia Project and the Educational Policy and Practice Study. For Jim Reineke's involvement and questions, I am deeply grateful. I am thankful for the wisdom and insights of Dan Chazan, Chris Clark, Susan Florio-Ruane, S. G. Grant, Claire Heidema, Nancy Jennings, Glenda Lappan, Sam Larson, Marilyn May, Lauren Pfeiffer, Dirck Roosevelt, Jimmy Spillane, and Suzanne Wilson. I am particularly grateful for Marilyn Cochran-Smith and Susan Lytle's interest in this manuscript, Kara Suzuka's ideas and creation of the original figures, and Carol Chambers Collins and Cindy DeRyke's assistance in its production. I am deeply thankful to Bill McDiarmid and Jay and Helen Featherstone, who encouraged and supported my intellectual risks. And heartfelt thanks go to David Cohen, for his vision of this work; to Deborah Ball, for hours spent helping me understand my own learning; and to Magdalene Lampert, whose commitment to my learning as a teacher and scholar made all of this possible. I give thanks to my parents and siblings, my first teachers, who helped me believe I could learn anything. I am grateful for the endless intellectual and emotional support of my husband, Steve Swidler, and the fresh perspective on learning offered by our son, Griffith. Steve and Griffith are the two people in this world who keep me centered so I can learn.

Introduction

I have a deep appreciation for the realities of teaching and learning to teach. After 9 years of successful elementary school teaching in a variety of grades and locations in the United States and abroad, I set out to learn to teach mathematics differently. I was intrigued by the possibilities of teaching mathematics in the conceptual and meaningful ways posed by the current reforms in mathematics education. Treating the teaching and learning of mathematics as an intellectual endeavor seemed to more closely resemble how I had come to see the teaching and learning of subjects like social studies and reading.

As a fifth-grade teacher in rural Vermont, in my seventh year of teaching, I encountered Man: A Course of Study (MACOS), a social studies curriculum developed by Jerome Bruner and his colleagues in the 1960s (Dow, 1991). Inquiry into what makes man human through comparative studies of salmon, herring gulls, baboons, Kalahari Bushmen, and Netsilik Eskimos organizes this year-long study. This was my first encounter, as a teacher, with an elementary curriculum that did not emphasize right answers. "Asking questions was to be as important as finding answers" (Dow, 1991, p. 79).

While teaching MACOS, I acquired a sense of the curriculum's structure as well as the culture of inquiry that drove it. I constructed connections between topics and relationships among themes, and learned to help children do the same. MACOS's many curriculum materials—numerous teacher's guides, booklets, films, and simulations—offered endless opportunities to engage children in the study of genuine questions lacking simple answers. I learned what it could mean to be engaged with children around real ideas and be intrigued, myself, by the content I was teaching children.

In my second year of teaching fifth grade, I turned my attention toward making reading instruction as interesting as social studies had become. Preparation for teaching reading shifted from deciding which pages to cover in a basal textbook to reading and discussing the text of real books and creating ways to teach comprehension skills within that context. Children had a variety of books to read and new classroom opportunities to communicate understandings of text through writing, art, and drama. I was awed by their abilities to represent their interpretation of text in multiple mediums. Reading and social studies fast became favorite subjects to teach.

While these curriculum changes were happening, however, my mathematics instruction remained untouched. I taught mathematics the way I had learned it through a year of college calculus. Whether I was the learner or the teacher, the routine was the same—memorizing rules and procedures, computing problems in silence, and checking answers with the teacher's guide. That I held such different views of teaching, depending on the subject, was not troublesome for me. Nor was it troublesome for the 22 fifth-grade teachers Stodolsky (1988) studied from 11 school districts in the Chicago metropolitan area. "When individual teachers shifted from one content area to the other, they varied cognitive goals, instructional formats, student behaviors, materials, and the extent to which pupils worked together" (p. 74). Stodolsky's description of math classes she observed held a mirror up to my own.

> Most of the classes we observed had competent teachers, but most of them seemed to hold a very limited view of what should be learned in school and appeared very skeptical of children's motivation and ability to learn. More often than not, students were treated as receptacles for knowledge that teachers transmit, not active participants in learning and the nature of knowledge to be transmitted, often defined by textbooks, and other curriculum materials, was chunked so small that its significance was not at all clear. (p. 135)

MOTIVATION TO CHANGE

Over the next 3 years as I continued to teach elementary school full time, I started and finished my master's degree in curriculum and instruction at the University of Vermont. While acquiring an advanced degree was my choice, my attitude was one of resentment at times. Who did these university people think they were to tell me the way things ought to be done in classrooms? As is true of faculty in many colleges and schools of education, many of the professors in the master's program had not taught in schools for years, if ever. I was skeptical of every theory presented, and confirmed or dismissed each one based on classroom experiences.

When I began full-time doctoral studies at Michigan State University, I hoped to become a different kind of professor. I had 9 years of teaching experience and was considered by others to be a good teacher.

(In my ninth year of teaching, I received recognition for outstanding elementary teaching through an award given annually by the University of Vermont.) I hoped that this background would enhance my credibility as a teacher educator and educational researcher. During my doctoral program, I worked as a research assistant on a project studying the relationship between policy (as set out in California State Department of Education, 1985) and practice in elementary mathematics education in California.[1] While it was refreshing and enlightening to learn of a new perspective on mathematics teaching and learning, part of me was distraught. I had entered graduate school thinking I was a good teacher. The credibility I thought I possessed was now questionable to me as I contrasted what my mathematics teaching had been to what I was learning it could be.

If I did not have some understanding of what it meant to implement these reform ideas about mathematics teaching in practice—my own practice—could I propose them as ideas for others to implement? This was certainly an alternative and one pursued by many people learning to be teacher educators—first, through graduate coursework, to read research and learn of ideas related to teaching, and later to teach these same research findings and ideas in teacher education courses. The strong tug of my identity as a teacher pulled me away from following that path. I needed to build consistency between my own teaching practice and what I would be teaching others about teaching.

Voicing this concern about my own credibility is potentially risky. It could raise questions about the practices of other teacher educators, many of whom do not have relevant or recent classroom teaching experience. Few university academics confront, head on, the fact that they teach others to teach and do research on teaching and learning, while remaining distanced, themselves, from experiences with teachers, students, and classrooms. In raising this issue, I do not mean to suggest that all teacher educators should become classroom teachers. Rather, I wish to insert a bit of humility into the role of university professors. In addition to the responsibility to teach students theory about teaching, we have a responsibility to learn what we can about teaching from practice, whether through our own work in schools or through the written accounts or close observations of other teachers' practice.

The issue of credibility is one that has surfaced in the past decade among educational researchers who have returned to the classroom (see, for example, Cazden, 1992; Cuban, 1990; Eisner, 1992; Hoffman, 1996; Lensmire, 1994). Cuban (1990) returned to the classroom because of similar issues of credibility, and I shared his desire to move between the worlds of theory and practice.

> I wanted to maintain my credibility both as a teacher and as an academic who writes about teaching and public schools. I believe deeply in the idea of a scholar-practitioner—that is, someone who can bridge the two very different worlds of the university and the public school. Such switch hitters are uncommon, and I wanted to be one of that breed. (Cuban, 1990, p. 480)

Eisner (1992) notes the nature of the gap existing between these two worlds. "There is a profound difference between knowing something in the abstract and knowing it through direct experience" (p. 263). I hoped a move back into the classroom would help to resolve this gap I felt growing within myself. I arranged to spend my second year of doctoral study (1989–90) teaching a fourth-grade math class. My teacher-self wanted to enact the vision of mathematics teaching and learning I was constructing through my work as a researcher.

A NEW VISION OF MATHEMATICS TEACHING AND LEARNING

The sources of my vision for what mathematics teaching and learning could be, at the time, came from the *Mathematics Framework for California* (California Department of Education, 1985) and the teaching practices of two colleagues: Magdalene Lampert (1987, 1990) and Deborah Ball (1993a, 1993b). In the years since, my vision of mathematics teaching and learning has been further strengthened by reform documents (National Council of Teachers of Mathematics [NCTM], 1989, 1991, 1995) and the California State Department of Education (1992). The ideas about mathematical knowledge, content, and learning underlying the reforms and Lampert's and Ball's practices seemed in stark contrast to my past views of the subject.

Mathematical Knowledge

Mathematical knowledge as conceptualized by current reforms is very different from the linear, sequential, fixed way I experienced it in my many years as a student and 9 years as a teacher: It is viewed as dynamic, constructed, and reconstructed through an ongoing process of sense making by the learner. It includes understanding how concepts are acquired and used. This means understanding the nature of mathematical argument or what counts as evidence and justification for a particular point of view. It also includes using and creating mathematical tools, language, and other representations to construct and communicate understandings of particular domains and the connections among them.

This view of mathematical knowledge does not entirely dismiss rules and procedures, but treats them as dynamic tools rather than static bits of knowledge. It places their use in the context of some purposeful activity where the short-term goal is for students to solve problems in meaningful ways and become mathematically literate. Sometimes, students use understandings of formal mathematical rules and procedures. Other times, they make use of intuitive understandings of mathematical ideas. However a problem is solved, the aim is for students to construct powerful and reasonable understandings of why particular solutions and problem-solving methods make sense.

Mathematical Content

The reform documents give curricular attention to particular content as well as mathematical processes. The California State Department of Education (1992) and NCTM (1989, 1991) provide lists of mathematical topics to be included in the elementary mathematics curriculum: estimation, number sense and numeration, number and number relationships, whole numbers, geometry and spatial sense, measurement, statistics and probability, fractions and decimals, patterns and relationships, and functions. While statistics and patterns represent topics new to elementary curricula, more traditional topics like long division are subsumed under whole numbers, decimals, fractions, or number and number relationships. Specific mathematical processes also are considered content by NCTM (1991) and include:

> Examining patterns, abstracting, generalizing, and making convincing mathematical arguments . . . definitions, examples, and counterexamples and the use of assumptions, evidence, and proof. Framing mathematical questions and conjectures, constructing and evaluating arguments, making connections, and communicating mathematical ideas. . . . (p. 133)

These topics and processes are intended to be taught in tandem, one providing the context for the other.

Learning Mathematics

The view of learning mathematics implied by the reform documents represents a "shift from learning mathematics as accumulating facts and procedures to learning mathematics as an integrated set of intellectual tools for making sense of mathematical situations" (NCTM, 1991, p. 2). Learning mathematics for understanding is seen as learning to represent and communicate a mathematical idea or interpret the mathematical representations of others, through the use of language, diagrams, pictures, manipulatives, and other tools to aid communication. It also entails learning particular models or structures of knowledge necessary to perform mathematical tasks. Understanding mathematics means building connections between procedural and conceptual knowledge. For many years, educators believed students had to learn basic skills and procedures before progressing to activities requiring conceptual understanding. Learning basic skills and how to reason through activities and problems with concrete materials and language as tools are integrated goals for all students in the current reforms.

The sense learners make of ideas plays a primary role. The reforms call for teachers to draw on children's intuitions or informal mathematical sense making and to have these ways of knowing be part of what is valued in school mathematics. This is based on a belief that the place to begin constructing meaning is with what the child knows, whatever form that knowledge takes. Learning occurs as students actively construct meaning for themselves by connecting new ideas with previous understandings. Making meaning out of mathematics is a social activity, and the reforms are based on the belief that "students' learning of mathematics is enhanced in a learning environment that is built as a community of people collaborating to make sense of mathematical ideas" (NCTM, 1989, p. 58). Learning mathematics is no longer viewed as the lone, silent practice of computation it had been for me.

IMPLICATIONS FOR IMPLEMENTATION

I tried to envision what the implementation of such ideas about mathematical knowledge, content, and learning in a math class actually would entail. Sections in the NCTM reform documents summarize the reforms, contrasting traditional and reformed instruction, curricular changes, and assessment practices. For example, the *Professional Standards for Mathematics Teaching* (NCTM, 1991) states the need for the following shifts in teaching and learning mathematics:

- toward classrooms as mathematical communities
- away from classrooms as simply a collection of individuals
- toward logic and mathematical evidence as verification
- away from the teacher as the sole authority for the right answers

- toward mathematical reasoning
- toward conjecturing, inventing, and problem solving
- toward connecting mathematics, its ideas, and its applications

- away from merely memorizing procedures
- away from an emphasis on mechanistic answer-finding
- away from treating mathematics as a body of isolated concepts and procedures. (p. 3)

I know all too well from my own teaching and learning experiences what this document advocates moving away from. These were prominent features of my past practice and probably typical of what Stodolsky (1988) observed. The difficulty is understanding in a practical way what to move toward and how to get there.

The *Curriculum and Evaluation Standards for School Mathematics* (NCTM, 1989) offers another set of expectations for change, as indicated in Figure I.1. There is not a one-to-one correspondence between the two columns in the figure. Therefore, the process of change is not as simple as eliminating one thing and doing something new in its place.

I could well understand the areas in which teachers were to decrease attention. They had been focal in *my* practice for years. What was less clear was what it would mean to "decrease attention" in these areas while "increase[ing] attention" in others. In many instances, to teach in these new ways meant decreasing attention to some aspect of my old practice while increasing attention in the direction of something I had never done before.

The Teacher's Role

Implied images of the teacher's role are plentiful. For example, *Reshaping School Mathematics* (National Research Council, 1990) describes the teacher as an "intellectual coach" (p. 40). The National Research Council (1990) proposes that at various times the teacher will be required to be a role model, a consultant, a moderator, an interlocutor, and a questioner. Teachers are to be "facilitators of learning rather than imparters of information" (California State Department of Education, 1992, p. 41). The NCTM (1991) imagines the teacher as musical conductor, someone who plays a central role in "orchestrating the oral and written discourse in ways that contribute to students' understanding of mathematics" (p. 35). Understandings of the role of the teacher continue to develop as researchers in mathematics education study teachers attempting to change their own mathematics instruction. For example, Simon's (1995) research describes in detail demands of the role of a math teacher creating a practice based on constructivism. Davis (1996,

FIGURE I.1: Teaching Practices to Increase and Decrease in Implementing the Math Reforms

Grade level	*Increased Attention*	*Decreased Attention*
K-4	use of manipulative materials cooperative work discussion of mathematics questioning justification of thinking writing about mathematics problem-solving approach to instruction content integration use of calculators and computers	rote practice rote memorization of rules one answer and one method use of worksheets written practice teaching by telling
5-8	actively involving students individually and in groups in exploring, conjecturing, analyzing, and applying mathematics in both a mathematical and a real-world context using appropriate technology for computation and exploration using concrete materials being a facilitator of learning assessing learning as an integral part of instruction	teaching computations out of context drilling on paper and pencil algorithms teaching topics in isolation stressing memorization being the dispenser of knowledge testing for the sole purpose of assigning grades

Source: National Council of Teachers of Mathematics. (1989). *Curriculum and Evaluation Standards for School Mathematics*, pp. 20–21, 72–73.

1997) uses the image of a listener to describe the role of the teacher he studied, and Clarke (1997) summarizes key components of the teacher's role based on analyses of others' research on teaching. While metaphors and descriptions put forth in theory or derived from empirical data are useful in imagining teachers' new roles, much more remains to be understood, from a teacher's point of view, about the depth and detail of the uncertainty and challenge faced by teachers learning to enact them (Schifter, 1996; Schifter & Fosnot, 1993).

The Demands of Change

Whatever the image or description, my sense was that learning to teach in these new ways was going to be hard. Others agreed. "The type of mathematics instruction that involves students actively and intellectually requires much from the teacher" (California State Department of Education, 1985, p. 13). Teachers who helped develop the *Mathematics Framework* (California State Department of Education, 1992) intended the following as some of the most difficult tasks confronting teachers in these reforms.

- change in how we practice our profession
- abandon traditional roles, become chief questioners and facilitators for students
- reflect, experiment, and accept uncertainty
- share doubts and confusions with colleagues
- through professional explorations and examination gain the experience and confidence necessary to implement the new programs and take the curriculum into our own hands (p. 12)

It remained unclear what it meant for any teacher to do these things in everyday practice. For example, what would it mean to "accept uncertainty" in a class of fourth graders? Or, what would it mean to "share doubts and confusions with colleagues?" The idea of revealing one's lack of knowledge to peers seemed so counter to the attributes of self-assurance, independence, and certainty valued in the culture of teaching (Feiman-Nemser & Floden, 1986; Lortie, 1975). The demands of making change seemed overwhelming and I had not even begun to teach. But what were my options? Without trying myself to actively teach mathematics for understanding, the best I could do was compare and contrast my sense of the scholarly ideas behind these reforms with my past, more traditional ways of teaching and learning mathematics. In theory, I could note the differences. Creating a practice would allow me to understand the process and problems in learning to teach mathematics differently from a teacher's point of view.

CREATING A PRACTICE

I taught only mathematics, 4 days a week, Monday through Thursday, during a 60-minute class period right before lunch, from September to December and March to June. In addition to teaching an undergraduate course on campus, I used January to March to take stock of my elementary math teaching experiences. I recognize that teaching only one subject and taking a break from teaching mid-year was in one sense a luxury. My schedule was quite different from the responsibilities of the typical elementary teacher. In another sense, my schedule was heavy: I was doing different and demanding jobs at once. I was a mathematics teacher, a researcher on teaching, and a teacher educator, and new at all three.

Setting

The class I arranged to teach was situated in one of many Professional Development Schools[2] working closely with Michigan State University. The norms for what it might mean for someone from the university to teach in an elementary classroom had already been established by my colleagues, Lampert and Ball, both of whom had been teaching math in this school for a number of years (Ball & Rundquist, 1993; Lampert, 1991). Influenced by these two teachers' practices within the school, many teachers had begun to enact similar visions of mathematics instruction in their classrooms. It was not necessary for me to convince anyone in the school that how I wanted to try to teach mathematics was a good idea.

The students in the school come from families where one or both parents are university students and represent an international population of many different nationalities and first languages. While the demographics of the 25 fourth graders with whom I worked were somewhat unique, I found a typical range of ability among them.

Textbook

I decided to use the math textbook adopted by the school district, the *Comprehensive School Mathematics Program* (CSMP) (Becker & Selter, 1996; McREL, 1986). Like most teachers who make use of textbooks, I did so with minimal support outside of what appeared in the text of the teacher's guide. The inservice component of CSMP had been done years earlier at the time of CSMP's initial adoption within the district. This curriculum was developed prior to the current math standards yet it promotes a consistent view of mathematics learning and teaching. It was developed with "dual emphasis on mathematical content and pedagogy designed to support mathematical reasoning" (McREL, 1992, p. 4). There are no actual student textbooks, only a detailed teacher's guide and student worksheets to accompany individual lessons, none of which contain rote practice of computation.

CSMP is built on the assumption that being mathematically literate is knowing something about calculus or understanding real numbers, the ideas of functions, and logic (CEMREL, 1981). Therefore, the purpose of the CSMP curriculum is to "give students an appreciation and feeling for algebraic structure." The concepts of set, relation, and function, without the formal mathematical terminology, hold a prominent place in this curriculum. CSMP is based on a conception of mathematics as a unified body of knowledge (McREL, 1992). From CSMP's perspective, mathematics is about ideas, not notation (CEMREL, 1981). Computation is still important but is introduced and practiced in the context of interesting problem situations intended to guide the sequencing of content and developing of computation skills (McREL, 1986). Mathematical content is organized into four strands: the World of Numbers, the Language of Strings and Arrows, Geometry and Measurement, and Probability and Statistics. Concrete representations, unique to CSMP (i.e., the Minicomputer, arrow roads, and string pictures), are used throughout.

The World of Numbers. The World of Numbers offers a variety of numerical experiences, including addition, subtraction, multiplication, division, negative numbers, decimals, and fractions. The Papy Minicomputer is a tool for representing numbers, performing calculations, and solving problems. It allows young children to work with relatively large numbers early on. It is a large square board divided into four squares of different colors and different values. Each smaller square within the large square has a different value—1, 2, 4, or 8. The values of the boards increase as their place in the base ten system increases (see Figure I.2). Checkers placed on squares have the value of the square. To calculate the number represented you add up the checkers' values. For example, the number on the Minicomputer shown in Figure I.3 is 16 or 2 + 4 + 10.

The Language of Strings and Arrows. The Language of Strings and Arrows is a tool for representing and studying sets and relations and using classification to understand concepts and solve problems. These are two nonverbal languages. The Language of Arrows is used to represent the mathematical concepts of relations and functions, numerical and nonnumerical relations like adding to, subtracting from, multiplying by, and sharing equally among. It also is used for logical

FIGURE I.2: The Values of the Minicomputer

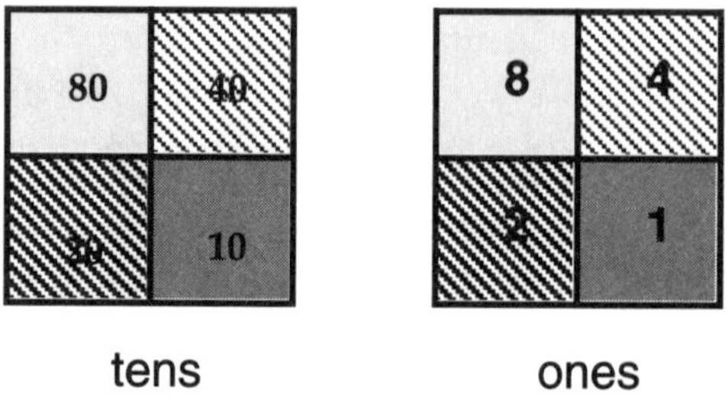

thinking activities. Children can "read and draw the relationship before they can present the same information in words" (McREL, 1986, p. vii) (see Figure I.4). The Language of Strings is used to represent the mathematical notion of set. Colored strings provide nonverbal language for classification, logical thinking, and deductive reasoning exercises (see Figure I.5).

Geometry and Measurement. In the Geometry and Measurement strand, measurement becomes a means for investigating problems and developing relationships between arithmetic concepts and physical concepts (McREL, 1986). Children have experiences with the metric system and geometric shapes, concepts, and spatial relationships.

Probability and Statistics. The strand of Probability and Statistics provides challenging problem situations and opportunities for students to think logically to predict the likelihood of future events.

FIGURE I.3: 2 + 4 + 10 or 16 as Represented by the Minicomputer

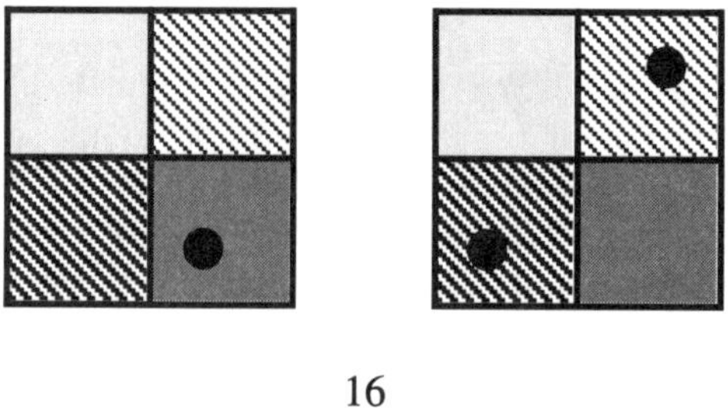

FIGURE I.4: An Arrow Road

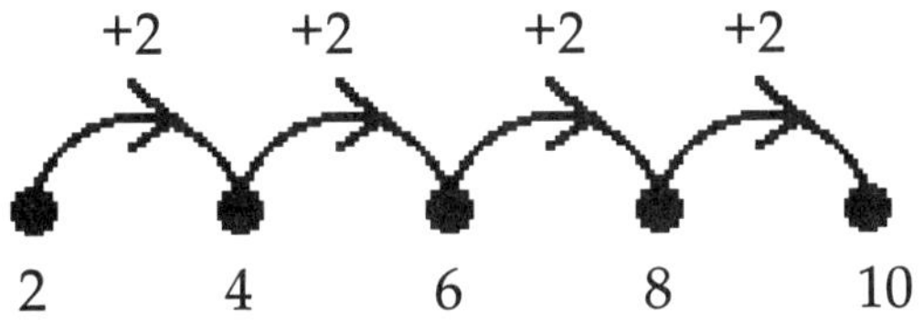

These four content strands are organized in a spiral with the intention that a lesson will be taught from a different strand each day. The spiral organization of curriculum "combines brief exposures to a topic (separated by several days before the topic appears again) with a thorough integration of topics from day to day" (CEMREL, 1982, p. 3). The continual introduction of, departure from, and return to topics and concepts are intentional and related to beliefs about learning. "The gap between the segments provides time for the material to 'sink in'; later segments proved a natural review of earlier segments" (CEMREL, 1982, p. 3). Learning is assumed to occur in a spiral, rather than a linear, process.

Colleagues

My teaching was situated in a complex set of relationships with three adults: the classroom teacher in whose classroom I taught, a university

FIGURE I.5: A String Picture

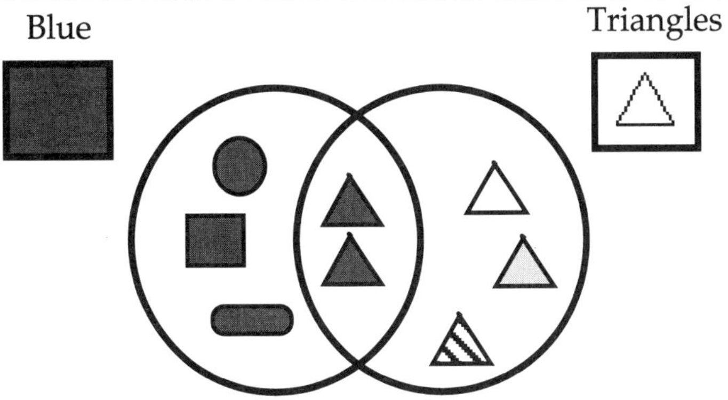

professor in the dual role of teacher and teacher educator who observed me on a regular basis, and a graduate student in educational psychology studying students' and my changing conceptions of mathematical knowledge (Reineke, 1993). The mere presence of three adults on a regular basis in my math classroom, for other than evaluative purposes, was something quite new for me and counter to the isolation and independence typically experienced by teachers (Feiman-Nemser & Floden, 1986; Lortie, 1975).

The relationship I had with the classroom teacher was one of mutual respect. We were both experienced teachers, she with a few more years of experience than me. We met weekly and focused our conversations on shared concerns: progress of individual students, pace of the whole group, and plans for the coming week. I drew on her wealth of knowledge about these children in and out of math class. I also benefited from her years of experience holding expectations for fourth graders and teaching math using CSMP. In addition to scheduled meetings, we informally shared our own observations about the day's lesson at the end of each class period (see Heaton, Reineke, & Frese, 1991, for further description and analysis of our work together).

As my feelings of dissatisfaction about my own teaching grew in my first year as a doctoral student, I sought out Magdalene Lampert, a university professor and elementary math teacher, and explained my desire to teach mathematics differently. From January to June, in the year before I took on the task of teaching fourth-grade mathematics, I met weekly with Lampert to view her math teaching on video tape or observe in her elementary math class. These were occasions to make sense of what Lampert was doing, compare and contrast it with my past practice, and construct an image for myself of the mathematics teaching I wanted to try to do. Although Lampert did not use the CSMP curriculum, her teaching was similarly focused on developing mathematical relationships and computation skills in problem-solving contexts. During the year that I taught, Lampert observed my mathematics teaching at least twice a week from September to December. Later in the school year, she observed, for a consecutive week. I also continued to observe her. She took notes each time she observed, which she later discussed with me. In these notes, she raised questions about my actions and intentions, pushed me to consider the mathematics I was trying to teach, and mulled over with me what students seemed to be understanding. Lampert described how she worked as a teacher educator based on her work as a teacher of children.

> The ideas that learners hold are to be respected, whether or not they match the teacher's or the expert's way of thinking about things. Both

> teachers and teacher educators who hold constructivist beliefs are thus faced with the challenge of respecting both where learners are coming from and where they want them to go. It seems duplicitous to respect children's ways of thinking about mathematics while not doing the same for experienced teachers' ways of thinking about teaching. (Heaton & Lampert, 1993, p. 76)

Jim Reineke, a doctoral student and researcher in educational psychology, observed twice a week, not necessarily the same days as Lampert, and talked with me about his observations on a weekly basis from September to December. He video taped all of the lessons, took field notes, and did informal interviews of students. I audio taped the lessons on the days when he was not there. He also interviewed me after each observation and tape recorded all of our conversations.

It was threatening having these three adults observe. To help ease the pressure of feeling like I might be judged by any one of them, we agreed that they each had a responsibility after each observation to help me make sense of what had transpired and contemplate with me what to do next. This meant the classroom teacher had to work with me as a peer, Lampert had to share what she understood about teaching, and Reineke had to alter his "objective" role as researcher.

STUDYING A PRACTICE

I made the decision to retrospectively study this year of teaching after recognizing the feasibility of such a study based on the variety of data that had been collected that year, assessing the reasonability of such a study based on a review of current research, and considering the potential contribution of a historical study of learning to teach by a learning-experienced teacher.

Feasibility

When I gathered together documentation of that year, in all its forms, I had a wealth of data from a variety of perspectives: my teaching journal, Lampert's annotations on all entries of my journal, Lampert's observation notes, video and audio tapes of my teaching between September and December, 3 weeks of video tapes of my teaching in April, an audio tape of a lesson in June, and audio tapes of interviews with Reineke between September and December. In addition, I audio taped "think alouds" for 3 weeks of my teaching in the spring. Figure I.6 summarizes the type and quantity of available data. While there are not

FIGURE I.6: Data Collected

Data Type	*Quantity*
video tapes of lessons	22
audio tapes of lessons	43
audio tapes of interviews with Reineke	19
teaching journal entries	97 days represented
Lampert's journal annotations	97 days represented
Lampert's observation notes	22 days observed
audio taped think alouds	12

all types of data for all days that I taught, I have my journal and Lampert's annotations as data for all days. For some days, other data sources overlap. The multiple perspectives represented in this collection of data allow me to challenge or affirm my own interpretations, and to triangulate my analysis (Hammersley & Atkinson, 1989).

Reasonability

In the current research on teaching mathematics for understanding, most seams are smooth between the intersection of mathematical knowledge and the various tasks of teaching. Some researchers, for example, have attempted to clarify what it means to teach mathematics for understanding from cognitive and sociological perspectives through an analysis of interaction (see, for example, Cobb, Wood, Yackel, & McNeal, 1992; Yackel & Cobb, 1996; Yackel, Cobb, & Wood, 1991). Others describe and analyze the dilemmas, decisions, and challenges they face within their own practices of teaching mathematics (see, for example, Ball, 1993a; Lampert, 1989, 1990; Schoenfeld, 1988, 1994). Still others have tried to understand teaching mathematics for understanding through studies of the application of understandings of learning to instruction (see, for example, Carpenter & Fennema, 1988; Hiebert & Wearne, 1988, 1992; Swafford, Jones, & Thornton, 1997).

A study of the bumps and bruises of my process of learning to teach allows for a particular view of how mathematical knowledge is used in the work of teaching, something that may go unnoticed in the smoother practice of more experienced teachers. As Shulman (1987) notes regarding the advantages of learning about teaching in the context of the practice of beginners: "The neophyte's stumble becomes the scholar's window" (p. 4). The rough edges in my work provide a more detailed view of the pathway of change than is available in the current research on teacher development in mathematics education (Fennema & Nelson, 1997).

The even and odd chapters in this book are paired. The inquiry I do in the even chapters is less like teacher research than the inquiry found in odd chapters. While both fit Cochran-Smith and Lytle's (1993) definition of teacher research, "systematic, intentional inquiry by teachers" (p. 5), my purposes for inquiry in the odd and even chapters differ. In the odd chapters, my purpose for inquiry is immediate and intended to help me in the day-to-day work of teaching. "The primary audience for the research is the teacher involved" (Burnaford, Fischer, & Hobson, 1996, p. 76). In the even chapters, the immediate need to teach is no longer present. Inquiry is now focused on answering the broader question of what a teacher needs to learn to teach mathematics for understanding.

Risks

The risk teachers face in studying their own classroom practices is well documented in teacher research literature (Burnaford et al., 1996; Cochran-Smith & Lytle, 1993; Fleischer, 1995; Hollingsworth & Sockett, 1994). "Teachers are not encouraged to talk about classroom failures, ask critical questions, or openly express frustrations. In short, the occupational culture perpetuates the myth that good teachers rarely have questions that they cannot answer about their own practices" (Cochran-Smith & Lytle, 1993, p. 87). While there is a history of mathematics educators studying their own practices (Ball, 1993a, 1993b; Lampert, 1989, 1990; Schoenfeld, 1994) and a tradition of autobiographical writing about teaching (Ashton-Warner, 1963; Calkins, 1983; Dennison, 1969; Eggleston, 1899; Kohl, 1967, 1984; Paley, 1979, 1981, 1990; Sprague-Mitchell, 1963; Stuart, 1949; Wiggington, 1986), these scholars use their practices primarily to study teaching, while my focus is to study teacher learning, specifically, my own learning as a teacher. To so openly reveal and examine my teaching and learning struggles leaves me feeling quite vulnerable, especially as I try to make a place for myself as a teacher educator and scholar, two roles traditionally associated with knowledge and authority about teaching.

In an effort to explain what is understood about classrooms, researchers sometimes write about the practice of particular teachers in ways that seem highly critical, somewhat offensive, and bordering on disrespect. Carter (1993), an educational researcher, disturbed by some researchers' accounts of teaching, wrote:

> In most conventional stories told about teachers, the narrator, however invisible, assumes a superior, more knowing attitude toward the characters. It is the narrator who has access to the relevant literatures, who frames the study, who provides the interpretations, and who modulates the teacher's voice. (p. 9)

Having written about another teacher's practice (Heaton, 1992), I know the dilemma faced by researchers trying to construct a narrative of a teacher's experience. It is challenging to know how to manage the examination of teaching in ways that respect the practitioner and the ideas being studied while also pushing at the status quo of theory and practice.

In this study, by using my own teaching and learning as objects of study, I escape the label of teacher basher. However, I risk being my own worst enemy by being extremely hard on myself. This is something I have battled throughout this entire study. I hope the strength of this book is in the ways it lets people see who I am as a learner, my process of learning, what it is I know, and what I have yet to learn. In moments of doubt, I have had to remind myself that revealing these facets of myself is worth doing. Eisner (1993), a scholar encouraging educational researchers to take such risks, warns, "Working at the edge of incompetence takes courage" (p. 10). I agree. In fact, sometimes more than I could muster.

NOTES

1. For findings from this research, see Ball, 1990; Cohen, 1990; Cohen and Ball, 1990; Heaton, 1992; Peterson, 1990; Prawat, 1992; Prawat, Remillard, Putnam, and Heaton, 1992; Putnam, 1992; Putnam, Heaton, Prawat, and Remillard, 1992; Remillard, 1992; Wiemers, 1990; and Wilson, 1990.

2. See Darling-Hammond (1994), Chapter 1, for a description of the Michigan Partnership, of which this school was a member.

CHAPTER 1

Do You See Any Patterns?

The first few weeks of school were wrought with difficulties and frustration. Repeatedly, I experienced a mismatch between what I hoped would happen and what actually happened. I began the school year relying heavily on the Comprehensive School Mathematics Program teacher's guide. The alternative was to do what I had observed several colleagues do, construct their own math problems for students (see Ball, 1993a, 1993b; Lampert, 1989, 1990). I was too scared to do that. In spite of years of teaching experience, I had the worries of a new teacher. Would I know what to do? Did I know enough mathematics? In theory, making use of the CSMP textbook seemed like a safe and sure way to begin my journey of change. In practice, however, efforts to make use of this new text quickly led to frustration.

TRAVEL PLANS

According to the teacher's guide, the title of the next day's lesson was, "Composition of Functions," a lesson from the CSMP Content Strand, World of Numbers. This title gave me little information about what to teach, what was to be learned, or what students were supposed to do. I could not recall any topic, chapter, or lesson in my 9 years of teaching that used this language. While functions had been a topic in my own learning of mathematics, what fourth graders were supposed to learn and how I was supposed to teach about them were not obvious to me.

In the past, there had always been a visible match between what the math textbook stated I was supposed to teach and what students were to learn and do. For example, long division was an algorithm with set rules and procedures to teach, and students practiced finding answers. Knowing when and what learners understood also was once more straightforward. Answers were either right and I moved on, or wrong and students did the work over. If many students had difficulty, I retaught the lesson. In the past, the mere title of a math lesson in the teacher's guide (e.g., two-digit division, three-digit multiplication, addition of fractions) gave me sufficient information to successfully plan, teach, and assess any lesson.

I turned to the summary at the start of the lesson in the CSMP teacher's guide.

> Using arrow diagrams and the Minicomputer, investigate the composition of certain numerical functions, for example, + 10 followed by + 2 and 3 × followed by 2 ×. (McREL, 1986, p. 11)

This generated more questions for me than it answered. I knew what it meant to find an answer, but what did it mean to investigate the composition of certain numerical functions? What was there to investigate? What was the role of arrow diagrams and the Minicomputer in these investigations? How was I supposed to assess what was learned in the investigation? Were there right and wrong ways to investigate? Finding the right answer had signaled completion of a task in the past. How was I to decide when an investigation was finished and it was time to move on?

To attempt to further understand what was meant by the phrase "composition of functions," I read through the content summary of the World of Numbers, in the section entitled Composition of Functions.

> Several lessons in this strand deal with what happens when you compose a sequence of functions, that is, apply the functions in order one at a time. These compositions lead to many general, powerful insights into the properties of numbers and operations. (McREL, 1986, p. xix)

What sorts of powerful insights were to be searched for and why? What constituted a "powerful insight"? I read further and found that fourth graders should have had previous experiences with composition of functions.

> Your students' extensive experiences with the composition of functions in the CSMP Upper Primary Grades curriculum led them to many insights that involved the development of algorithms, the discovery of number patterns, and efficient mental arithmetic techniques. A goal in this strand is to review these discoveries and to apply composition to new situations and problems. (McREL, 1986, p. xx)

That students might be familiar with the content was of some comfort. Even if I could not see the point of the lesson, maybe they would.

Most CSMP lessons were designed to be completed in a single class period. I found, however, that lessons took much longer than CSMP or

I planned. It was only a few weeks into the school year and I was already worrying about falling behind. A sense of responsibility for covering curriculum was nothing new. I experienced it each year I taught. However, with experience, I had learned which parts of the text I could confidently and responsibly skip and how to set and reorder priorities under the pressures of time. My judgments about pace were off. This was unsettling. I no longer trusted my own discretion. Consequently, I clung to the teacher's guide. In those first few weeks, I experienced a strange sense of falling behind in a context in which I was unsure of where I was supposed to be going.

I did begin to modify individual lessons but kept with the sequence of lessons in the textbook. CSMP typically allowed 1 day for each lesson, while I spent at least 2 days, sometimes longer, on each one. I looked for logical ways to divide the single-day CSMP lessons over a couple of math classes. For example, this lesson on functions involved a set of problems around addition, subtraction, and multiplication. I decided to do the three problems that dealt with addition and subtraction (see Figure 1.1) one day, and the problems that dealt with multiplication the next. Even with splitting up this lesson, I remained skeptical whether I could cover it all. The table seemed easy enough for students to complete. Students would find starting and ending numbers; identify the composition arrow, an arrow that would encompass the other two; and notice patterns in the relationship between inputs (starting numbers) and outputs (ending numbers). I decided to work the first problem together and assign the remaining two problems to be done independently.

My plans, while textbook-driven, were mathematically and pedagogically aligned with my new image of mathematics teaching and learning. For example, patterns are a mathematical theme throughout reform documents, and large- and small-group mathematical discussions are a central feature of any mathematical pedagogy rooted in social constructivism (Simon, 1995; Steffe & D'Ambrosio, 1995; Yackel & Cobb, 1996) and theories of doing mathematics based on mathematical argument (Lakatos, 1976). Given my observations in Lampert's class and reading of the *Mathematics Framework* (California State Department of Education, 1985), I knew the question of patterns in the script of the CSMP lesson was an important one and a discussion of patterns was a way to consider mathematical relationships. I had regularly observed Lampert engage fifth graders in discussions of patterns. I wanted the opportunity to attempt such a discussion myself. Before I became acquainted with the reforms, I never knew there was anything that would lend itself to a discussion in math class. I was

FIGURE 1.1: Exercise 1 in the Teacher's Guide

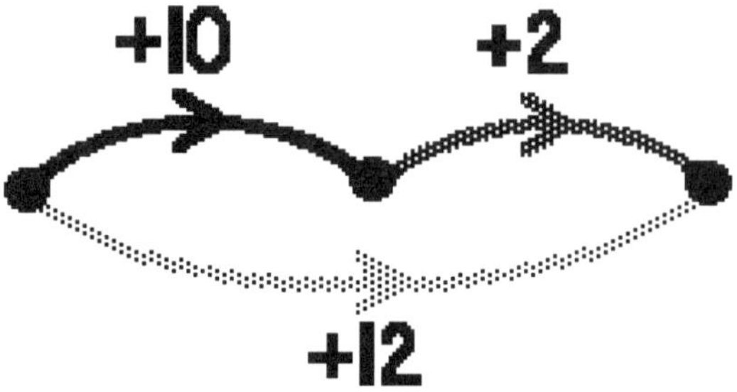

starting number	ending number

Source: CSMP for the Intermediate Grades, Part I (1986), pp. 12, 16. Reprinted with permission of McREL, 1999.

learning I could ask students to explain how and why they solved a particular problem in a particular way. I had led discussions in other subjects and could not imagine that mathematical discussions would be that much different to conduct. While had I never spent much time talking about patterns in math class, they were an everyday idea and part of everyday language. I assumed that noticing patterns in a table of numbers would not be much different or more difficult than any everyday occasion for noticing patterns (e.g., in nature or fabrics). In theory, a discussion of patterns seemed manageable.

MEANINGLESS PATTERNS

To begin class, I wrote a problem on the chalkboard (see Figure 1.1)—I left out the + 12 arrow included in the teacher's guide. I said, "I'd like you to take a look at the chart. Think of a number. Just think of a number and add 10 to it and then add 2 more to it." After a few moments of silence while students thought of numbers, I asked someone to propose a beginning number. I called on Richard, whose hand was in the air.

> *Richard:* 99.
> *Ms. Heaton:* And what did you end with?
> *Richard:* 111.
> *Ms. Heaton:* And can you tell us how you got that?
> *Richard:* Well, I did 99 plus 10 equals 109 and then plus 2 is like 9 plus 2 equals 11.

The first four pairs of numbers were contributed by different students. Asking students, "How did you get that?" was my idea. It was not in CSMP but was a question I had heard Lampert ask to prompt discussion among fifth graders. However, individuals, like Richard, responded with procedural explanations that did not seem to hold anyone's interest. Why was this happening? Whenever Lampert asked the question, students always offered interesting explanations.

As the teacher's guide suggested, I varied the process of filling the table with numbers by asking some students to give ending numbers first, followed by an explanation of how they generated them. The teacher's guide also suggested calling on someone different to offer these explanations. These variations appealed to me. I thought that starting with the ending number might make the explanations about how students got from one number to the other more interesting, and calling on a variety of students might help the talk seem more like a discussion. Here is a sample of the interactions.

> *Ms. Heaton:* Can somebody give us their ending number? The number they ended with, David?
> *David:* 19.
> *Ms. Heaton:* And what was your starting number?
> *David:* 7.
> *Ms. Heaton:* Can you tell us how you got that?
> *David:* Because 7 plus 10 is 17 and 17 plus 2 is 19.
> *Ms. Heaton:* O.K., can someone else give an ending number? Jennifer?
> *Jennifer:* 215.
> *Ms. Heaton:* Can someone else tell us what she might have started with? Bob?
> *Bob:* 203.
> *Ms. Heaton:* O.K., how did you get that?

Bob: Because 203 plus 10 is 213, 213 plus 2 is 215 and I have another number.

I continued until I reached the bottom of the chalkboard (see Figure 1.2—The crossed-out number was an error in computation). We created a table of numbers but efforts to generate a discussion led nowhere. Disappointed with the lack of interesting talk, I held high hopes for the activity of noticing patterns. I followed the script in the teacher's guide, which ran like this:

T: Look closely at this chart. What patterns do you notice?
S: An ending number is always larger than the starting number.
S: If you start with an even number, you end with an even number. If you start with an odd number you end with an odd number.
S: An ending number is always 12 larger than the starting number. (McREL, 1986, p. 14)

FIGURE 1.2: Numbers Contributed by Students

starting number	ending number
99	111
8000	8012
250	262
1	13
7	19
203	215
~~4088~~ 4988	5000

I said, "I want you to look at these numbers. Do you see any patterns?" For 15 minutes, students gave ideas about patterns and I listened for ones that matched the teacher's guide. I called on Valerie first. She said, "Each of them have a beginning number and then they have an ending number that is 12 more." I asked how she knew the ending number was 12 more. She said, "Because you have to add 10, you find a number, you add 10 to it and then 2." I added the bottom composition arrow as in the teacher's guide (see Figure 1.1), and said, "If I were to put in another arrow here, what would I put, plus what?" Valerie responded, "Plus 12." I added the label to the arrow and, given my goal to initiate a discussion, continued to find out what others were thinking.

Pili said, "I see, I think I see a pattern. It is 80, 80." She pointed to the "80" in 8000 and the "80" in 8012 as she said, "80 right here and 80 right here." (See Figure 1.2)

Hearing Pili's idea, I questioned myself. Surely, we were looking for patterns more significant than what she noticed. In an everyday sense of patterns, she was right. These were 2 four-digit numbers and the first two digits in each were 8 and 0. Taken together, however, they did not mean "80." The 8 was really 8000 and the zero was in the hundreds place. In another attempt to promote discussion, I asked for comments on Pili's idea. This call was a pedagogical move I had observed Lampert make. Besides being able to explain their own ideas, I wanted students to listen and build on others' ideas. Pili's response seemed like a meaningless pattern. I hoped a classmate might challenge her.

I continued with words I often had heard Lampert ask, "Okay, what do other people think about that?" I called on Jennifer, who said, "I agree with her." Unfortunately, this was not the response I wanted. I hoped Jennifer would disagree with Pili. I could have asked Jennifer why she agreed with Pili but I was not in a mood to hear explanations for what I thought was a meaningless pattern. Was it not clear that Pili was wrong? Should I just tell her so? But would not that be counter to students constructing their own meanings? How did the categories of "right" and "wrong" fit into my desire to give students space to make their own sense of ideas? Should I even accept responses I thought were wrong? Did any of their responses link to the mathematical point of looking for patterns? What I am struggling with is what Prawat and Floden (1994) refer to as the "constructivist's dilemma." I am trying to be open to students' ideas as well as true to the mathematical ideas that are important for children to learn. My own uncertainties about the mathematical ideas in this lesson add to the already complex balancing act created by this dilemma.

I moved on without pursuing Jennifer's comment or dealing with the issue of right and wrong answers. I addressed the class, "Okay, are there any other patterns that you see?" I called on Lucy, who said, "There is 8 and then 8 going across and then 2 and then 2 going across." She approached the chalkboard. She pointed to the 8s in 8000 and 8012 and the 2s at the beginning of the pairs of numbers, 250, 262 and 203, 215 (see Figure 1.3). Again, in a visual sense of pattern, she was right. These numerals matched one another, but how did this observation relate to patterns in the context of functions? Reluctantly, I returned to Pili, who was waving her hand frantically, ready to give another "pattern." She said, "I see three zeroes here and here," and she underlined the three zeroes in 8000 and 5000. I was worried. This "pattern" seemed even more irrelevant than her last one. Maybe I should have said what I thought of her ideas. She attempted to draw connections between a pair of numbers not in the same row. Since the ordered pairs were generated independent of one another, there was no mathematical reason why there would be meaningful connections

FIGURE 1.3: Lucy's Patterns

starting number	ending number
99	111
8000	8012
250	262
1	13
7	19
203	215
~~4088~~ 4988	5000

between numbers not found in the same row. Maybe Pili would see for herself the unreasonableness of her idea, if I could get her to talk about it. I asked her to explain. She said, "In 8000 there are three zeroes and in 5000 there are three zeroes." But what did this have to do with patterns? What was a pattern? What I was hearing were not patterns. Jennifer followed Pili's comment and said, "I have something similar to hers but it is not exactly the same." She approached the chalkboard and underlined the zeroes in the hundreds place in 8000, 8012, 4088 (the crossed-out figure), and 5000.

On the one hand, I was excited that a student had listened to another and was attempting to build on a classmate's idea. On the other hand, I was growing frustrated as I watched one irrelevant pattern lead to another. In fact, Jennifer had just included a number that did not even belong on the chart. It was there with a line through it because it had been revised. The idea of taking all ideas seriously, revised or not, was something else I had picked up from Lampert. Seeing Jennifer making use of the error, however, made me question my decision not to just erase it as I would have done in the past. Keeping it here just added to the confusion.

These were the least of my worries. I was searching for mathematical sense in students' responses, but was this an instance where there was none to be found? I was curious how Jennifer would describe the pattern she noticed, so I asked, "What would you say that pattern is? How would you describe it?"

> *Jennifer:* One here and one here, and one here and one here.
>
> *Ms. Heaton:* I don't understand what you mean by one here, what are you showing me?
>
> *Jennifer:* There is a zero in the hundreds place and one zero in the hundreds place, and there is one zero in the hundreds place and one zero in the hundreds place.

Hearing Jennifer talk of place value provided a momentary sense of relief. I continued to ask myself whether what she or other students were saying had to do with patterns or functions. What was a meaningful pattern? What was a function? I called on Richard. He explained, "I have another pattern. Can I go up there? Right here is three zeroes in a row (8000) and three ones in a row (111), and then three zeroes (5000) in a row." I asked what the pattern was. He said, "000, 111, 000." I was troubled as I listened to Richard. These were not patterns in a mathematical sense but what were they? And, what were mathematically meaningful patterns in this table of numbers? Students noticed "patterns" in pairs of numbers in the same row, pairs of numbers that spanned rows, and now senseless patterns in each of the columns. "Meaningful" patterns could not be found in columns generated by beginning or ending numbers chosen at random.

When I could bear this "discussion" no longer, I announced, "I want to move on to another example." I wrote a new problem on the chalkboard (again using a sample from the teacher's guide). I knew that I had already made plans to teach the second half of this lesson the next day. Could I bring myself to come back the next day and face the question of patterns again? I left school perturbed with myself for having trusted the teacher's guide, annoyed with myself for having thought I entered this lesson prepared to teach, and confused about the mathematical meaning of pattern.

LOST WITH A GUIDE

That evening, I was distraught and troubled by the day's events. My mind was filled with questions. Was I teaching? Were students learning? Why was I unable to get an interesting discussion started? Why was I asking students about patterns anyway? What was a pattern? Did the students' patterns have any relevance? What is a function? Later that day, in my interview with Reineke, who had observed the lesson, I said:

> I felt as if I was floundering today . . . I was asking myself the question, what do I mean by a pattern? What does the word pattern mean? I am not sure I have an answer to these questions but that's what I was thinking as I stood up there, listening to these kids. And the sort of student responses the book says will come up—that CSMP puts in, what kids would respond when you say, "What's a pattern?"—none of that came up. I felt really as if I didn't know what to do to move a discussion about patterns. (Reineke interview, 09/20/89)

I had planned a reasonable lesson. I had trusted that the teacher's guide was going to help me through it. It was letting me down. It was, at once, too much and not enough of a guide. It had given me enough guidance to lead me to believe we could do this activity even though I failed to acquire any broader sense of its purpose. In the midst of teaching, I found myself lost with a guide.

As soon as I heard students' responses, I realized I did not know what I meant by "pattern." I had not considered that there might be a mathematical sense of patterns that was different from other, more familiar notions. I also did not understand why I was asking the question. I initially asked the question because it was in the teacher's guide and, given what I knew about the reforms, it had seemed consistent with my goals. It frustrated me to have an intuitive sense about what was not a pattern but no real sense for what constituted mathematically sound ones.

The predicted responses in the teacher's guide were not useful. I had these responses in hand when I entered class. In the past, I would have been intent on listening for them. If I had not heard them, I would have encouraged students to produce these "right" answers. Like many good "traditional" teachers, I have had years of experience asking convergent questions, leading students to the "right" answer. But in this situation, while I listened for particular responses, I also wanted to be open to the idea that students' answers might vary from the teacher's guide. I did not realize the uncertainty this would create. How was I to know which students' responses were reasonable variations of the responses found in the script and which were not? How was I supposed to respond to these variations? Was there a way that I could be respectful of all responses and at the same time let students know that many of their observations were irrelevant to the question of patterns in this mathematical context? The script in the CSMP teacher's guide was designed with questions for me to initiate but I was frustrated by the little help it offered in figuring out what to do next in the situation, especially when what students said did not match the script I had before me.

My frustrations went beyond thinking students' responses did not match the teacher's guide. I was bothered that the talk during class felt out of my control. Moreover, I did not have any sense of what it would mean for it to be *in* my control. I wanted to do something to guide a discussion but, not knowing what to do, remained silent. Inside, I was struggling. I knew that we were not having a meaningful discussion yet I did not know what we could have talked about or how I could have shaped what individual students were saying into one. While troubled by students' responses to the question of patterns, I also was wrestling with my own response. I repeatedly asked myself a question neither asked nor answered in the teacher's guide but nevertheless on my mind—what is a pattern?

Had I been more certain of the point of the lesson, I might have been more willing and able to move away from the script and ask students a different question—*my* question—or I might have had a way of responding to their responses. As it was, the script in my hands, intended to help me in my teacher role, felt disconnected from students and myself and the sense anyone was making of the question of patterns.

Questioning the Directions

When I asked students to notice patterns, my response was to ask myself, "What is a pattern?" I never considered asking students this question. I was surprised when Reineke brought up the idea in our interview.

> *Heaton:* The question for me became what is a pattern? And, are these things that the kids are giving me patterns?
> *Reineke:* So, why didn't you ask that?
> *Heaton:* Why didn't I ask—?
> *Reineke:* The class.
> *Heaton:* What?
> *Reineke:* What is a pattern?
> *Heaton:* That would have been a good question. That is the question that I had on my mind.

How could it not have occurred to me to see this as a reasonable question in the situation? I did not even consider it an option. Why? One reason might have had to do with my concern for time and my own need to get through the lesson I had planned. How could I have justified spending time on what patterns were when, according to CSMP, students were supposed to be searching for them? The teacher's guide outlined the task to be one of noticing, not defining, patterns. Would students have gotten through the task of noticing patterns if we had stopped to define them? I began, however, to question how worthwhile the task of noticing patterns had been without some shared understanding of what we were looking for and why. A similar question, "What is a whole number?" comes up in a lesson a week later (Heaton and Lampert, 1993). These are questions whose answers seem, on the surface, to be obvious. When grounded in real practice or the particular understandings of a roomful of children and my own understandings, anything one might assume as obvious quickly falls by the wayside.

I was relieved to find out that Reineke similarly had asked himself about the definition of patterns. Lampert also had observed this lesson and as I read her observation notes for the day, I saw that she also had been mulling over the definition of a pattern. What follows is an excerpt from her notes:

> Asking "do you see any patterns?" What do you want to get out of that? Was the idea to get someone to say that the ending number is 12 more than the beginning number? There are relevant and irrelevant patterns (i.e., like 8-2-2 and 8-2-2). Hard to exactly explain what I mean by "irrelevant patterns." There *are* things you could get out of almost every pattern the kids come up with . . . what the kids are saying are more like *observations* than *patterns*. I think you were trying to get at this a bit when you asked, "Does that pattern apply to any other set of numbers?" (Lampert observation notes, 09/20/89)

Lampert's notes illustrate the complexity. The definition of a pattern is related to questions of relevance. Questions of relevance are related to questions of purpose, and questions of purpose are related to the mathematics (i.e., *both* mathematical ideas and ways of knowing) to be learned. How might things have turned out if I had asked the question that made sense to me rather than the one found in the teacher's guide, which held little meaning for me? Would spending time defining patterns along with searching for them have been a waste of time?

The question of patterns was legitimate but to see it as such means valuing an interpretation of a mathematical task as a worthwhile part of doing mathematics. It requires viewing directions as open to interpretation, and solutions as dependent on assumptions about the task. That is, noticing patterns and being able to justify why something is or is not a pattern, depends on shared understanding of the definition of pattern in a particular context. Seeing the question, what is a pattern, as legitimate also means learning to feel all right about asking genuine questions. I had learned to ask questions for which I did not have the answers in social studies but I had never experienced this in mathematics. In social studies, my own curiosities and desires to learn more about the question at hand were central to my role as a teacher. Up to this point in math class, however, every question I asked had a right answer found within the teacher's guide. I began teaching this year worried that I lacked sufficient mathematical knowledge. Reality hit when I faced a mathematical question for which I really did not know the answer. Could I ask students a question that was genuine for me? Admitting to others and myself that I had something to learn clashed with my view of my role and responsibilities. I was the teacher. I was supposed to ask students questions for which I had the answers. Or was I? It seemed irresponsible to continue and pretend I understood. But how could I admit the need to learn in a professionally responsible manner? To spend time on understanding directions would slow down moving through the textbook. I needed to convince myself this was all right. In addition, I needed to learn to set aside the teacher's guide, value what I did not know, and trust myself to ask a different question—my own question—even if it meant raising questions about directions in the teacher's guide.

Seeing the Limitations of Following a Guide

My frustrations with using the teacher's guide prompted me to reconsider why it was I thought following this teacher's guide was initially a good idea. Since I wanted to move away from "traditional" teaching, "nontraditional" curriculum materials seemed like a useful tool for making fundamental changes in my view of content as well as how to teach. I was coming to see that making the changes I desired in my teaching was not going to be as easy as merely following the CSMP teacher's guide as I had followed teacher's guides in the past.

I also began to question the adequacy of the teacher's guide as it was written. Were there ways the teacher's guide could have better prepared me for this lesson? Were there ways to situate the math problems in broader mathematical goals that I might have understood? Were there aspects of teaching that neither CSMP nor any other textbook could prepare me for? I was frustrated with the script format of the guide. It offered me one possible route through the material. At the time, I thought there was a complete mismatch between the anticipated student responses in the teacher's guide and what students said. In my journal I wrote:

> What kids came up with did not resemble these responses . . . I am wondering what the role of the teacher's manual is in this type of teaching. Much space in CSMP is taken up with examples of student and teacher interactions. I'm not finding this particularly useful and at times troublesome. When I read it, I think I have an idea of what is going to happen in class and today was an example, last Thursday was too, of things not going as I anticipated. I base my plans on the book but that doesn't seem to be working. (Heaton journal, 09/20/89)

Before this year, in the midst of such felt confusion, I would have steered students back on the course defined by the textbook, regardless of their responses. Now, however, I wanted to do things differently.

What sort of guide could give me enough of a feel for where I was headed to guide decisions about what to do next yet do so in ways that would allow me to be responsive to particular students' ideas?

Understanding What Is Worth Noticing

Alongside frustrations with patterns, I was discouraged by my attempts to generate a discussion. Even though students were talking, both as they filled the table with numbers and as they searched for patterns, little of the talk was meaningful. I knew the discussion was flat and irrelevant but I was at a loss for how to change it. Teaching as telling dominated my past practice as a teacher. At the time of this lesson, only a few weeks into the school year, I was determined to change my ways of interacting with students and avoid doing anything that resembled telling. Asking questions was a way to make this happen. I even inserted questions of my own into the script of the teacher's guide. There was still no discussion.

Given my lack of success at generating a discussion, I began to consider that there had to be more to my role than just asking questions. There was something to learn about commenting on students' ideas in the situation to fuel a conversation; how to decide what to say, about what, to whom, and when. The questions—Do you see any patterns? How did you get it? What do others think?—along with the questions in the CSMP guide had gotten students talking. But then what? Asking the questions was one thing. Knowing what to do with the responses was quite another.

If I had known why we were looking for patterns, I might have been able to consider the relevance of students' patterns. When I asked about patterns in my journal, Lampert commented in the margin, "Isn't a larger question, why are we looking for patterns in math class in the first place???" (Lampert annotation of Heaton journal, 09/20/89). This is similar to the question I asked when I started planning for this lesson. I tried to figure this out from the information given in the text. When I was unable to, I dismissed the need to know based on experiences as a math teacher. I assumed I could teach even if I did not quite understand the purpose of what we were doing. I could just follow the textbook. In practice, I found it to be not quite this easy.

CAUGHT BETWEEN THE OLD AND THE NEW

In this lesson, I find myself in the midst of change somewhere between abandoning my old ways of teaching mathematics and embracing a new vision of practice. In this transition, I am frustrated, confronted by much that I still need to learn while simultaneously carrying the responsibility for teaching. I find myself trying to understand mathematical content while helping others learn it. Specifically, I am trying to understand patterns and composite functions and the importance of these mathematical ideas in the elementary curriculum. I am trying to learn what it means to generate a discussion in mathematics while attempting to lead one. I am trying to learn to use a new textbook while feeling dependent on it. Learning to teach mathematics differently as an experienced teacher is not a matter of putting one's current practice on hold, learning a new pedagogy, re-entering the classroom, and doing things differently. The learning process is not nearly so simple, linear, or clear-cut. Rather, it is inherently complex, messy, and uncertain, embedded in and dependent on teaching.

This lesson and my reflections begin to illustrate the ways in which it is possible for a teacher to learn from experience. I move forward with new insight into what it is that I need to learn based on analysis of what I did not understand. For example, not understanding the mathematics I was aiming to teach led to an increased awareness of the need to comprehend the mathematical purposes of activities I give children and questions I ask. I have a new appreciation for the need to understand the mathematics I want children to learn, but still wonder exactly what mathematics I need to know. Fumbling around for what to say or do as I attempted to lead a mathematical discussion helped me to see that my constant questioning during the lesson was not the only change I needed to make to shift away from my former role as teller. I found myself in the midst of unfamiliar content with a familiar tool. Blindly following the teacher's guide in unfamiliar mathematical territory was not working. What would a new relationship with the textbook look like? Through inquiry into the absence of my own mathematical understandings and the nature of my struggles to teach mathematics differently, I begin to see deep connections between mathematics and pedagogy. My inquiry continues.

CHAPTER 2

Learning to Comprehend Mathematical Ideas in Topics, Texts, Tasks, and Talk

At least part of my frustration when I taught the pattern lesson was directed at the teacher's guide and my perception of its inability to help me respond to students. To understand what it is that I might have known that would have contributed to greater continuity between the image of teaching I wanted to be doing and my teaching practice, I re-examine my frustrations. Specifically, I try to better understand my relationship with the textbook—what I expected of it or what I thought it would do for me, the trust I had in it and the people who wrote it, and the way I made use of it. I want to better understand the mathematical ideas inaccessible to me within the CSMP text, invisible to me in the task, and inaudible to me in students' responses when I taught the lesson.

LEARNING TO RECOGNIZE AND UNDERSTAND THE MATHEMATICS

My efforts to understand the relevance and meaning of patterns and functions in this particular lesson are part of more general efforts to understand the mathematical ideas fundamental to children's learning of mathematics, whatever the topic. Exploring fundamental mathematical ideas entails drawing on understandings from books and people in concert with my own reasoning to try to understand the nature of the mathematics to be learned, the importance of these particular mathematical ideas in the discipline of mathematics, the place of these ideas within the K–12 curriculum, and how children make sense of these ideas.

Why Spend Time on Patterns?

Mathematics is a science of patterns, and a search for patterns drives the work of mathematicians. Steen (1990) writes, "Seeing and revealing hidden patterns are what mathematicians do best" (p. 1). Reformers advise a similar search for patterns by all students at every grade level. For example, the *Professional Standards for Teaching Mathematics* (NCTM, 1991) note that as "teachers shift toward the vision of teaching presented by these standards, one would expect to see teachers asking, and stimulating students to ask, questions like 'Do you see a pattern?'" (p. 4). Patterns, according to the *Mathematics Framework* (California State Department of Education, 1992), "help children to see order and make sense of underlying structures of things, situations, and experiences. Patterns help children predict what will happen" (p. 108). The *Curriculum and Evaluation Standards for School Mathematics* (NCTM, 1989) connect patterns to a study of functions.

> From the earliest grades, the curriculum should give students opportunities to focus on regularities of events, shapes, designs, and sets of numbers. Children should begin to see that regularity is the essence of mathematics. The idea of a functional relationship can be intuitively developed through observations of regularity and work with generalizable patterns. (p. 60)

The study of patterns bears strong resemblance to the work of real mathematicians. It permeates the *Mathematics Framework* (California State Department of Education, 1992) as a "unifying idea" across content strands.

> What matters in the study of mathematics is not so much which particular strands one explores, but the presence in these strands of significant examples of sufficient variety and depth to reveal patterns. By encouraging students to explore patterns that have proven their power and significance, we offer them broad shoulders from which they will see farther than we can. (Steen, 1990, p. 8)

What Is a Pattern?

Pattern is a word that carries common understanding in everyday language as well as particular meaning and relevance in the world of mathematics. The danger with this is that one may assume the meaning of words like this is the same in either context and meet difficulty transferring the everyday meaning to the mathematical situation. Given my familiarity with the word *pattern*, I had no reason to question its meaning until I got into the middle of the lesson. While familiar with the everyday use of the word *pattern* in describing the design in fabrics, for example, I was less familiar with its mathematical meaning and relevance. Leinhardt, Zaslavsky, and Stein (1990) offer examples of several other such words and reasons for potential difficulties: "Words such as *line* and *point* have particular meanings in both natural language and mathematical language; the meanings both overlap and misalign with each other" (p. 51).

It appears that the authors of the textbook assumed the mathematical meaning and relevance of the word *pattern* were obvious. There was no indication in the teacher's guide that my question about what a pattern is, was reasonable. There was no explanation. For me to have questioned the meaning, would have required me to value my own question above what I found in the teacher's guide, to teach with a kind of confidence I did not possess at the time. Viewing the CSMP teacher's guide as the exclusive authority on what and how to teach was the safest way to proceed, although, in retrospect, perhaps not the wisest. I assumed that the teacher's guide knew better than I what questions I should be asking. At the time, I also assumed that questioning the definition of a pattern was related to my inexperience with "investigations." I realize now that noticing and defining mathematical patterns are related tasks within an investigation. Contemplating one informs the other.

Regularity and predictability are two fundamental characteristics of a pattern. Something is a pattern if regularity is observable. Regularity allows one to be predictive about the pattern's behavior. A numerical pattern with regularity and predictability enables description of a relationship between two variables. Identifying a pattern enables manipulation of one variable and simultaneous prediction of another. A relationship between two variables with this kind of regularity and predictability is a function.

What Is Function?

A function is a relationship between sets. If for any member of one set, it is possible to describe the predictability that enables identification with certainty of the corresponding member of a second set, then the relationship between the two sets is a function. In other words, given $f(x) = y$, for any x ($x_1, x_2, x_3, \ldots$), any y ($y_1, y_2, y_3, \ldots$) is predictable.

Leinhardt, Zaslavsky, and Stein (1990) offer a similar explanation of this relationship using slightly different language. A function is a "special type of relation or correspondence, a relation with a rule that assigns to each member of Set A exactly one member of Set B" (p. 27). A well-defined function allows one to say what *y* value will go with a particular *x*. For each *x* there is only one value of *y*. Each element in the domain (Set A) corresponds to only one element in the range (Set B). When starting with a particular value, one can predict with certainty the output. Functions carry with them the notion of predictability and regularity, the essence of pattern. However, not all patterns are functions.

Why Spend Time on Functions?

Understanding the composition of functions encourages students to look flexibly at numbers. Studying functions in elementary school is preparation for algebra or "the study of operations and relations among numbers through the use of variables" (Karush, 1989, p. 4). It is also preparation for operating "with concepts at an abstract level and then applying them, a process that often fosters generalizations and insights" (National Council of Teachers of Mathematics, 1989, p. 150). CSMP is a curriculum oriented around functions. It builds conceptual understanding of algebra through the use of arrow roads. From this foundation, the expectation is that, in later grades, students will be able to do the type of abstract generalizing required in the explicit study of algebra. A major goal is to help develop the kind of flexible thinking that will ease a transition to the more advanced world of mathematics, especially aspects of mathematics having to do with functions; for example, "the geometric image of a graph, the algebraic expression as a formula, the relationship between dependent and independent variables, an input–output machine allowing more general relationships and the modern set-theoretic definition" (Tall, 1992, p. 497).

An overall goal of CSMP and this lesson was to learn to look at calculation in different ways. Composing functions offers practice with mental strategies for the purpose of combining different numbers. For example, adding 12 can be seen as adding 10 plus adding 2. A developer of CSMP admitted that the problems given in the CSMP teacher's guide, +10 followed by +2, +7 followed by –3, and +9 followed by –4, are not particularly strong examples of good practice in mental arithmetic. The numbers are easy to calculate; complex mental computation strategies are unnecessary. As it was, the mental strategies students shared were neither interesting to those reporting nor intriguing for those listening. Larger and more difficult numbers to compose would have made completion of the table more interesting and the goal of developing mental computation strategies more obvious.

LEARNING THE PURPOSE OF THE TASK

What is the meaning of the task of searching for patterns in a table? Why are tables useful in learning about functions? What were students supposed to notice when looking for patterns in the table? These were not questions I asked myself when I taught the lesson. At that time, I hoped that by doing the lesson, students would learn something. Someone else had decided it was a worthwhile task.

Why Search for Patterns in a Table?

I approached my investigation of the meaning of the task of searching for patterns in a table with two questions in mind. First, what sort of representation of a function is a table? Second, what does it mean to look for patterns within a table and what does it contribute to a K–12 curriculum? I drew on two colleagues, both of whom are mathematics educators, knowledgeable about middle and secondary school mathematics, and interested in curriculum development, to analyze the task of filling in the charts and noticing patterns from a mathematical perspective.

Recall the problems under the heading "composition of functions" in CSMP (see Figure 1.1). The labels of the arrows varied. Once the table was filled with numbers, the students were to notice patterns. To complete the table, students chose inputs and predicted outputs or chose outputs and predicted inputs. Picking any starting number, they could be certain of the ending number by adding 12 to it. They also could predict the starting number by subtracting 12 from any ending number. The only uncertainty came if a student had difficulty with the computation. When students started with the ending number, they performed the inverse function, arrived at by subtracting first 2 and then 10. Doing enough of these, students could have learned about inverse relationships among functions. Commutativity is also a possible focus. The students could have asked, if the two functions are applied to a starting number in the opposite order, do you get the same ending number? In other words, does +2 followed by +10 result in the same number as +10 followed by +2? The table normally is thought of as the simplest representation of a function. In the example +10 followed by +2, the table represents a composition of functions. The first operation, add 10, gives an output that becomes the input for the second operation, add 2. The first function is $f(x) = x + 10$. The output of this function is symbolized by $f(x)$. The input is x. The second function is $g(x) = f(x) + 2$ where $f(x)$ is the input for $g(x)$. It can be written algebraically as shown in Figure 2.1. In the case of the composition of functions, the two functions are composed such that the outputs for the first function become inputs for the second function.

What Is the Relationship Between Patterns and Functions?

Looking for the kinds of patterns that lead to an understanding of functional relationships involves multiple steps as well. The two columns of a table come in rows with a beginning number and an ending number. The beginning number determines the ending number because the labels of the arrows enable the prediction of an ending number from a beginning number, or vice versa. To notice patterns, as they relate to functions, one makes observations about a pair of numbers in one row. If these observations hold true for more than one row, they are patterns.

There is another layer of sophistication to the analysis of patterns in tables. In a table where the starting and ending numbers are not

FIGURE 2.1: **The Beginning and Ending Numbers Generated by Students, Represented Algebraically**

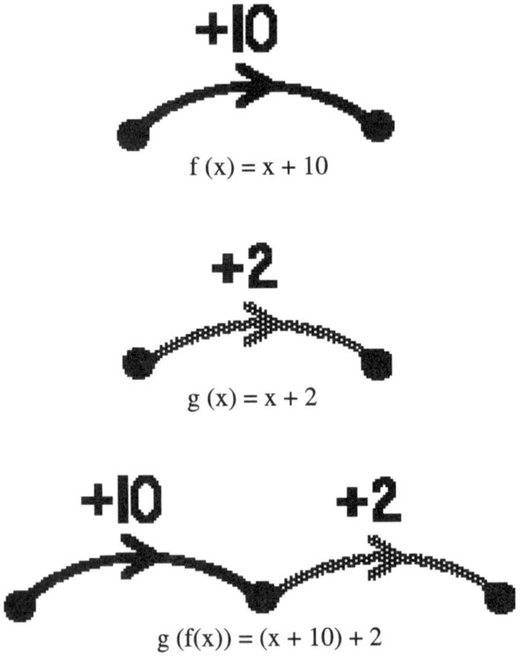

chosen randomly, as in Figure 2.2 where the starting numbers are intentionally all multiples of 3, patterns may be found by looking down columns as well as across rows. By putting the beginning numbers in order, and choosing them with some regularity, one can make use of patterns in the column of starting numbers to predict the column of ending numbers. Since outputs depend on inputs, one can look to see if there are patterns in the change of outputs when there is an orderly change in inputs. Is there a constant difference between outputs when there is a constant difference between inputs? Patterns in a table where the numbers are ordered and not randomly chosen have the potential to be more complex because they represent a coordination between changes in inputs and outputs. Patterns and functions are also a way to consider classification. Functions are objects and as objects they can be classified and sorted. Different functions will have different kinds of patterns. For example, the function + 12 has certain patterns. The functions + 10 and + 2 will have other patterns.

LEARNING TO MAKE SENSE OF STUDENTS' UNDERSTANDINGS

What sense can be made out of the question of looking for patterns in the context of a table of numbers? How did I understand responses in the teacher's guide and those that came from students then and what

FIGURE 2.2: Starting and Ending Numbers as Multiples of 3

starting number	ending number
3	15
6	18
9	21
12	24

is my understanding of them now? Again, my aim is to understand discrepancies between predicted student responses and what students actually did. When I examined discrepancies in the previous chapter, it was to figure out what to do next in teaching. Here the purpose of a reexamination of these discrepancies is to try to better understand what I needed to learn or what I could have known that would have enabled me to make sense of students' responses. In my explorations of the intentions of CSMP through conversations with one of the developers and an analysis of student responses within CSMP, I discovered a wealth of mathematical ideas and connections within the teacher's guide that were not apparent to me at the time I taught the lesson.

One may question the necessity of doing an analysis of a textbook in the context of a study of learning to teach. While my study represents a journey of learning to teach differently, it is also a study of what one needs to learn to teach mathematics differently. This is where the analysis of my use of a textbook is relevant, for it points to important things to understand about the content and process of learning to teach mathematics for understanding. Mine is not the study of the implementation of CSMP. For a study of the implementation of particular mathematics textbooks, see Remillard (1996).

Why Particular Student Responses in the Teacher's Guide?

I focused my conversation with a developer of CSMP on the three student responses listed in CSMP in response to the question of noticing patterns (see the left column of Figure 2.3). When I taught the lesson, I assumed these responses were ones I should expect from students because these represented how others have responded to the question. What I discovered from my inquiry is that student responses appearing throughout CSMP come either from the developers' experiences in classrooms with students or represent mathematically interesting ideas from the perspectives of authors responsible for writing the text of the lesson. The responses in this particular lesson were mathematically interesting ones and not ones that I necessarily could expect from students. Had the teacher's guide included information on the origin of these responses and why they were considered mathematically interesting, my expectations before and during the lesson might have been different.

I am now able to see mathematical significance in each of the responses. The third response in the text, that the ending number is always 12 larger than the starting number, is a generalization and most closely related to the function notion. This response represents an im-

FIGURE 2.3: CSMP Student Responses Compared with Actual Lesson Responses

The CSMP Script	Transcript 09/20/89
T: Look closely at this chart. What patterns do you notice?	Ms. Heaton: OK, I want you to look at these numbers, do you see any patterns? Valerie?
S: An ending number is always larger than the starting number	Valerie: *Each of them have a beginning number and then they have an ending number that is 12 more.*
S: If you start with an even number, you end with an even number. If you start with an odd number, you end with an odd number.	Ms. Heaton: O.K., and how do you know that it is 12 more?
S: *An ending number is always 12 larger than the starting number.*	Valerie: Because you have to add ten, you find a number, you add ten to it and then 2.
(McREL, p. 14)	Ms. Heaton: If I were to put in another arrow here, what would I put, plus what?
	Valerie: Plus 12.

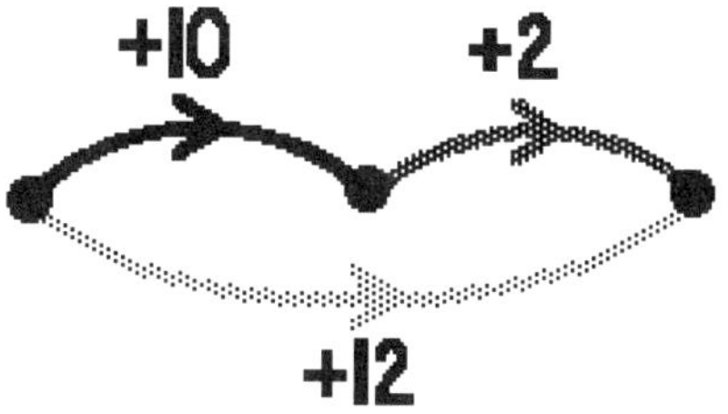

portant mathematical idea through its description of the relationship between the starting and ending number. The first response, that the ending number is always larger than the starting number, is an observation that is a more general variation on the third response. The second response, if I start with an even number, I end up with an even number, or the parity of the odd/even relationship of the starting number and ending number, is an interesting observation. If I add 11 rather than 12, the parity would be different. The significance of each response and how they are related to one another is something I have learned, but not from the teacher's guide. If I had known any of this going into the lesson, would it have helped me along the way? At this point, I can only hypothesize that the answer to this question would be yes.

Questions of how much, what kind, and in what ways to provide information for teachers plague curriculum developers, including the developers of CSMP. When I voiced concern about limited access to certain information and ideas through the teacher's guide, the CSMP curriculum developer countered with the concern that giving teachers too much background on the responses would make the use of the guide too tedious. What is the balance between enough and too much information in a teacher's guide? In this particular example, how useful are suggested students' responses without the additional information I learned on my own? I expected students' responses to vary, but without an understanding of the significance of the mathematics, I had no idea what constituted reasonable variations.

What Were Students Seeing?

What am I able to see and hear in students' responses now that I was unable to see or hear at the time I was teaching? I was curious to see if it really was the case that what my students had said in response to the question, "Do you see any patterns?" was unlike any of the students' predicted responses in the teacher's guide. I replayed the video tape of this lesson with the scripted lesson from CSMP in one hand and a transcript of the lesson in the other.

Valerie's Response. Looking back at the teacher's guide and transcript now, I see that Valerie, the first person to respond to my question of patterns, actually gave one of the answers found in the teacher's guide. Her response, recorded in the right-hand column of Figure 2.3, matches the last predicted student response in the CSMP guide. I even responded to her, added the composition arrow, and labeled it with plus 12. Yet, I continued with what resulted in a pointless discussion of patterns and ended class frustrated that students had not responded in any of the ways predicted by the teacher's guide. What does this discovery of the similarity of Valerie's comment to what appears in the teacher's guide say about what I understood to be my frustrations at the time and what I have since learned that might help me to understand these frustrations? My aim is to understand rather than discount the sense I made out of the situation at the time. How could it be that I thought students' responses to the question of patterns were meaningless and bore no resemblance to what was in the teacher's guide, when Valerie's response was a close match to the one in the text?

One explanation that comes immediately to mind was my focus on having a discussion. If this was the case, then I was not really focused on the right answer and it might make sense that I did not "hear" Valerie or want to "hear" her. If I had, she was the first person to respond and her "right answer" might have ended the discussion. What more was there to talk about? It also seems quite possible that I might have "heard" Valerie but did not really understand what she was telling me. At the time, I was uncertain about the point of the lesson. If the question of noticing patterns relates to reasons why one would look for them, it might follow that I was listening for responses in the teacher's guide but I did not really understand their significance to the question of patterns in this context. I did not really know what I was listening for. My ability to hear Valerie now may have something to do with what I have learned about patterns and functions since that year of teaching.

Another explanation may be found in the work of Davis (1996, 1997), who makes important distinctions among the kinds of listening a teacher must learn to do. With teacher's guide in hand at the time I was teaching, I compared what I heard with what I saw in the script before me. I was "evaluating the correctness of the contribution by judging it against a preconceived standard" (Davis, 1997, p. 359). Davis probably would agree that I was listening *for* something in particular, in ways similar to Wendy, a middle school mathematics teacher with whom he worked. "Wendy's listening seems to have been constrained by the fact that she was listening *for* something in particular (i.e., mathematical explanation) rather than listening to the speaker" (Davis, 1997, p. 359). When I replayed the tape, long after the fact, I had a much more appreciative way of listening. I was focused on listening *to* what was said rather than listening *for* something in particular.

Valerie's response, that each of the beginning numbers has an ending number that is 12 more, seems on the surface to be rather mundane. But I am now able to appreciate its mathematical significance. Her response is a generalization that defines the composition of the two functions in this problem. If she had been asked to write down what she was saying in the shortest form possible, she probably would have written something like, "number + 12." This could be thought of as the expression, "$x + 12$." Looking for patterns in a table is like looking for a relationship that can be used to define a function which matches the data in the table. This is a move in the direction of algebra. Valerie's generalization meets the criteria of regularity and predictability, two key characteristics of patterns. It is a statement that holds true for pairs of numbers in all rows. One could choose any starting number and predict with certainty, using Valerie's pattern, the ending number.

Other Students' Responses. What about other students' responses? Were those patterns? If not, what were they? Students' observations were not mathematically relevant patterns. The students were observing regularities in numbers. Take the "pattern" a student noticed, that there are 3 zeroes in 8000 as well as in 5000 (see Figure 1.3). There is nothing predictable about this observation. It does not indicate relationships among other numbers in the table. If I use the criterion that to find patterns I must start out with observations about a pair of numbers in one row, responses where students made observations about pairs of numbers not in the same row are eliminated immediately as patterns. Even when students were looking at pairs of numbers in the same rows, the sorts of regularities they were noticing were not predictive.

Students gave procedural explanations of how they found beginning and ending numbers to fill in the table. These explanations, which I first interpreted as dull and pointless, reveal the meaning of the composition of functions and the relationship between outputs and inputs.

> *Richard:* Well, I did 99 plus 10 equals 109 and then plus 2 is like 9 plus equals 11.
> *Lucy:* 1 plus 10 is 11 plus 2 is 13.
> *David:* Because 7 plus 10 is 17 and 17 plus 2 is 19.
> *Bob:* Because 203 plus 10 is 213, 213 plus 2 is 215.

If their procedures were represented in a chart of inputs and outputs, they would look as they appear in Figure 2.4. Perhaps there was something interesting to notice in their responses. Mathematically, the composition of functions is a layer of complexity that is quite significant, even though the mental arithmetic necessary to fill in the chart in this particular lesson was rather simple for fourth graders.

FIGURE 2.4: The Relationship Between Inputs and Outputs

input	*output*	*input*	*output*
99	109	109	111
1	11	11	13
7	17	17	19
203	213	213	215

MARK TWAIN: ANOTHER VIEW OF THE TERRITORY AND TOOLS FOR TRAVEL

Twain's experiences learning to navigate a riverboat as described in *Life on the Mississippi* (1883/1990) parallel my beginning adventures making change in my practice. Naive preconceptions of the work, continual struggles with learning to do the work, and insights into what one needs to know to be able to navigate are themes found throughout Twain's story: "I supposed that all a pilot had to do was to keep his boat in the river, and I did not consider that that could be much of a trick, since it was so wide" (p. 38). Twain's simple view of the work from the shore seems comparable to the simplicity and ease with which the idea of teaching and learning to teach mathematics for understanding is written and talked about through the eyes of many advocates of the current reforms in mathematics education. On the Mississippi River, from behind the wheel of the boat, Twain came to have a different understanding of the work. He quickly realized that learning to be a riverboat pilot was not merely a matter of learning to keep the boat afloat on what looked from the shore to be a predictably wide body of water. The ever-changing river and the sort of understanding needed to navigate it required his continual attention.

In this particular lesson, I found myself dependent on the CSMP teacher's guide. I trusted that it was going to help me do the kind of mathematics teaching I envisioned. In a similar way, Twain began his adventures on the river dependent on a notebook: "I had a notebook that fairly bristled with the names of towns, 'points,' bars, islands, bends, reaches, etc.; but the information was to be found only in the notebook—none of it was in my head" (Twain, 1883/1990, p. 43). We both envisioned a text as the key to navigating unfamiliar territory. We both became frustrated. Within a short time on the river, Twain found that the information in his notebook was insufficient for actually piloting the boat on the river. Likewise, in the act of teaching, I recognized the limitations of the teacher's guide. Twain (1883/1990) wrote of the frustration his reliance on his notebook caused him.

> The boat came to shore and was tied up for the night . . . I took my supper and went immediately to bed, discouraged by my day's observations and experiences. My late voyage's notebook was but a confusion of meaningless names. It had tangled me all up in a knot every time I had looked at it in the daytime. I now hoped for respite in sleep; but no, it reveled all through my head till sunrise again, a frantic and tireless nightmare. (p. 48)

I had similar feelings. The teacher's guide and the sense I made of it seemed to hinder more than help. I was naive to think that the teacher's guide could carry aspects of this teaching that I was learning were my responsibility.

Mr. Bixby, Twain's teacher, knew much more about the river than Twain realized, and I doubt that Mr. Bixby, an experienced riverboat pilot, ever imagined that Twain would rely so heavily on his notebook. Similarly, I do not think the developers of CSMP ever expected me to cling so tightly to the text. But to stray from the text in purposeful ways, without wandering too far from important mathematics, I needed a much stronger and clearer sense of purpose for what I was doing. I needed to understand the mathematics from a disciplinary, child's, and curricular point of view. I started out searching for that when I planned the lesson. When I failed to turn up much that seemed useful, my experience pushed me to go ahead with the lesson anyway, only to soon find myself unprepared and ill equipped.

Twain (1883/1990) summarizes what he learned about the way he needed to learn the river.

> I have not only to get the names of all of the towns and islands and bends, and so on, by heart, but I must even get up a warm personal acquaintanceship with every old snag and one-limbed cotton-wood and obscure wood pile that ornaments the banks of this river for twelve hundred miles; and more than that, I must actually know where these things are in the dark. (p. 47)

That he learned he needed a "personal acquaintanceship" with the river seems related to what I am learning about the personal relationship I need to acquire with the mathematics I am trying to teach. After Twain had spent some time learning particulars about the river, Mr. Bixby spoke in more general terms about what it means to know the river: "You learn the shape of the river; and you learn it with such absolute certainty that you can always steer by the shape that's in your head, and never mind the one that's before your eyes" (Twain, 1883/1990, p. 54). This way of knowing the river is similar to how I imagine more knowledgeable colleagues, like Ball and Lampert, know the mathematical terrain they navigate with students, independent of any teacher's guide. But I am still learning the river.

CHAPTER 3

The Teaching Has Been Missing

Even though I took lesson plans directly from CSMP, not much of what happened went as planned. Everything seemed "out of synch." I had been following a teacher's guide yet felt lost. I had the urge to move forward but lacked a clear sense of direction. I wanted to engage students in a mathematical discussion but did not know what to talk about. I trusted the teacher's guide but had little confidence in myself and was uncertain whether and what students were learning. I was going through the motions of teaching but doubted that anything I had done in these first 3 weeks of school resembled teaching mathematics for understanding. I had expected changing my practice to be difficult but never imagined it would be this hard.

THE NEXT DAY

As I prepared for the next day's lesson (the second part of Exercise 1), questions and difficulties that arose in the previous lesson (see Chapter 1) weighed heavily on my mind. I searched the teacher's guide, and was thankful to find no mention of patterns in the second half of the lesson. I reread the lesson summary I had tried to understand several days earlier.

> Using arrow diagrams and the Minicomputer, investigate the composition of certain numerical functions, for example, + 10 followed by + 2 and 3 × followed by 2 ×. (McREL, 1986, p. 11)

I was no clearer about the point of this lesson as I looked it over a second time. What were students supposed to investigate about the composition of functions in the context of multiplication? Why was the Minicomputer used in this part of the lesson and not the previous one?

The arrow problems looked similar to those in problems the day before and, again, students could complete them without understanding the point of the lesson. In one example, the left top arrow was marked

3 x, and the right one 2 x; I turned the page in the teacher's guide and saw the composition arrow (the bottom arrow) labeled 6 x for this particular problem (see Figure 3.1). Initially, I labeled it 5 x rather than 6 x, adding 3 x and 2 x. I wondered if students would do the same thing.

I planned to assign a CSMP worksheet that included problems like these as well as ones like those done the day before. The paper-and-pencil task of completing a worksheet would provide a way to evaluate students' learning. My mounting uncertainty might be eased if students did well. A worksheet also gave me a purpose quite familiar to my past mathematics teaching for getting through the lesson. A mathematical purpose for understanding these problems was neither clear nor necessary.

The Minicomputer

The Minicomputer, a CSMP tool described earlier (see Introduction), was intended to be used for working problems in this part of the lesson. However, there was no explicit discussion in the teacher's guide about why. Its presence implied its importance and I constructed my own rationale. Arranging checkers on the Minicomputer illustrated the number of groups involved in the multiplication process. Knowing the number of groups was essential to correctly labeling arrows, which was something students had to do on the worksheet. For example, multiplication of 14 by 3 is the same as 3 groups of 14 objects or 42. Fourteen can be represented on the Minicomputer with 1 checker on the 10 square and 1 on the 4 square or 10 + 4 (see Figure I.2 for the values of each square on the Minicomputer). Three times 14 or 3 groups of 14

FIGURE 3.1: The Composition of 3 × and 2 × is 6 ×

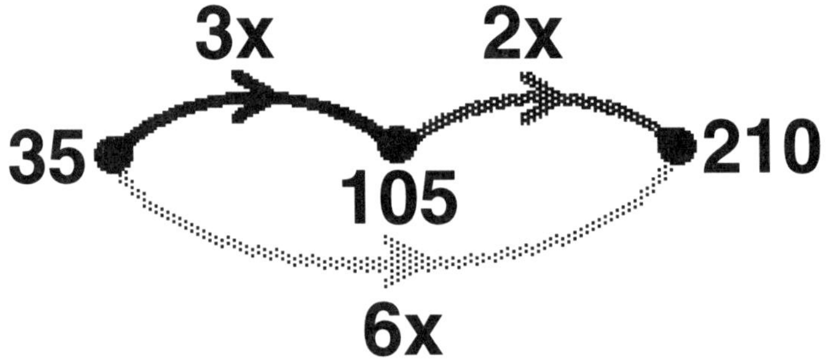

can be represented by repeating the pattern for 1 group of 14, 3 times. Multiplying this quantity by 2, or doubling it, means the same as 2 groups of 3 groups of 14 or 2 x (3 x 14) or 6 x 14. This can be represented on the Minicomputer by repeating the pattern of checkers used to represent 3 x 14, twice (see Figure 3.2). This repeated pattern in the physical arrangement of checkers used to represent 3 x 14 was not

FIGURE 3.2: Repeating Patterns of Checkers to Represent 3 × 14, Twice

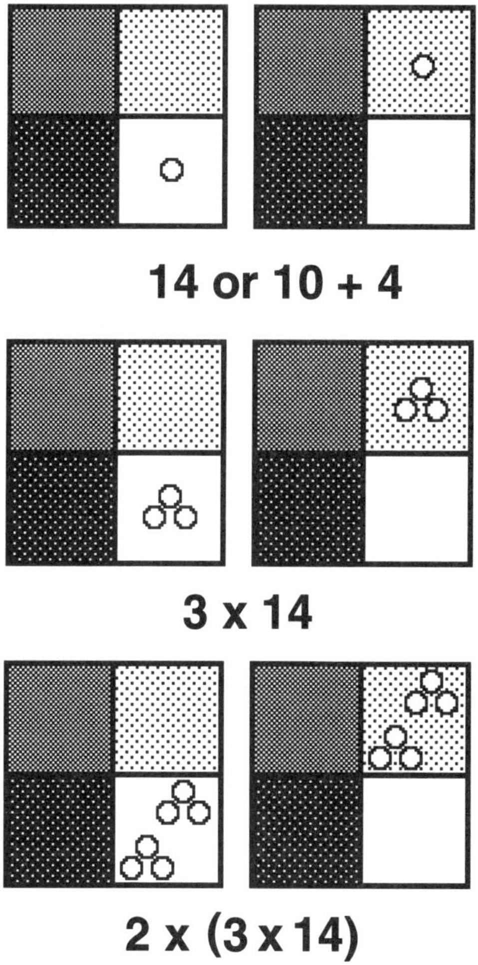

something discussed in the CSMP teacher's guide. It was my way of making sense of using the Minicomputer in this context.

I clung to how problems were worked in the teacher's guide and insisted the Minicomputer be used for every problem. The Minicomputer was still a new tool for me as well as the handful of students in this class who were new to the school and CSMP. We had used the Minicomputer just once before. It was challenging to consider the placement of the checker, the value of the square, and the arithmetic necessary to keep a running total of the checkers used. My own reluctance to take on the required mental computation encouraged me to give problems straight from the textbook and copy the placement of the checkers as they appeared in the guide.

Following the Script

I started math class by placing three checkers on the Minicomputer to show 49 or 40 + 8 + 1. I read from the script and asked what was represented on the Minicomputer. John responded, "49," and at my request explained how he knew: "Because the checker on the purple space on the second Minicomputer [in the tens place] is 40, and the other ones Minicomputer [in the ones place], that has a checker on the 8 and 1 on the ones and that is 9." I moved on to the next problem and asked students to show "double 49." Bob volunteered (see Figure 3.3). His arrangement of checkers matched the teacher's guide. The teacher's guide, however, contained this additional note.

FIGURE 3.3: Double 49

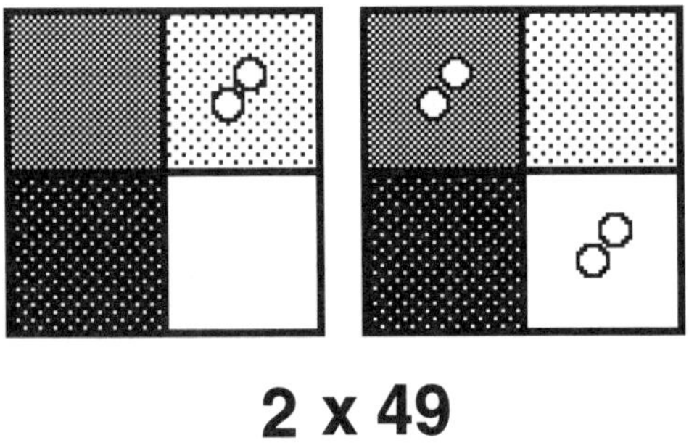

NOTE: There are other correct configurations for 2 x 49, such as the standard configuration for 98, but the one above emphasizes that there are 2 49's on the Minicomputer. (McREL, 1986, p. 17)

There was no explanation, however, as to why the configuration emphasizing two 49s was preferred over other arrangements, such as the one Mike suggested with the least checkers possible: "I have an easier way of doubling 49 than just putting another checker on the 40s and another checker on both the 8 and the 1." He arranged checkers as shown in Figure 3.4. This was easier if the purpose of using the Minicomputer was to show the solution once it had been computed by some other means. It missed the point if the Minicomputer was intended to represent the number of equal groups.

It was becoming part of my routine to ask if others had ways of thinking about the problem. Ron explained his mental strategy: "50 and 50 is 100 and then take away 1 and it is just 99. And, then another 1 and it is 98." Outwardly, I accepted all responses whether they matched the teacher's guide or not. Inwardly, my frustrations mounted. Some students, like Ron, were not using the Minicomputer and others were using it to show the total rather than illustrate the process. It was going to become harder to make it through my plans if students kept offering these alternatives. I continued to use the Minicomputer as an accompaniment throughout the lesson, even though I was one of the few people in the class engaged in its use.

FIGURE 3.4: 98 With the Fewest Checkers Possible

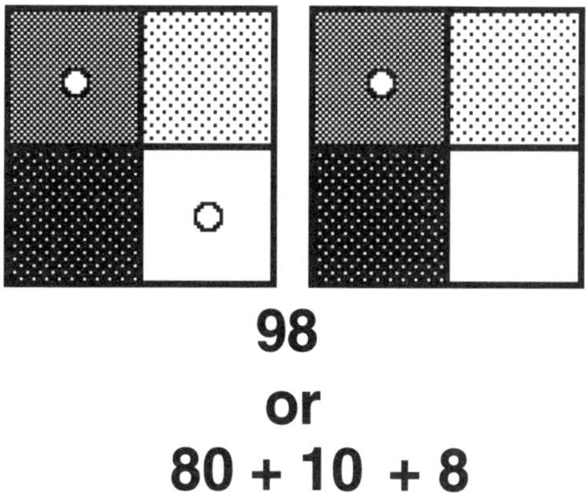

I worked the next two examples from the teacher's guide with the numbers 65 and 27. I arranged checkers to represent these numbers and then prompted students to double or triple the pattern of checkers to represent 2 or 3 times the number. Arranging the checkers in repeating patterns to illustrate the process was painstakingly slow and of little interest to those who had already figured out the answer by some other means. Most students preferred sharing mental strategies for finding an answer, or arranging checkers to represent the answer with the least checkers possible. An interest in repeating patterns of checkers on the Minicomputer continued to be more mine than theirs.

The next problem began like the others. I arranged a number on the Minicomputer (see Figure 3.5). Sipho explained how he knew this was 35. "Because there are 2 checkers on the tens board. One of them is on the 2 and the other is on the 1: 1 plus 2 equals 3. And on the ones board you have a checker on the 4 and there is another checker on the 1: 4 plus 1 equals 5." I assumed he meant 30 when he said "3" on the tens board. I asked Jamila to show 3 times this number. She carefully repeated the pattern of checkers for 35, 3 times, under my direction. Jennifer, who had been doing mental computation and paying little attention to the checkers and Minicomputer, announced that she knew the answer was 105 and explained how she knew: "Because I did it in my head again. I went 5 plus 5 plus 5 is 15, put down 5 carry the 10, 30 plus 30 plus 30 equals 90, and I would add one more 10 and that's 100." She, like many other students, had no reason to believe the Minicomputer was an important tool when she had mental strate-

FIGURE 3.5: How Do You Know This Is 35?

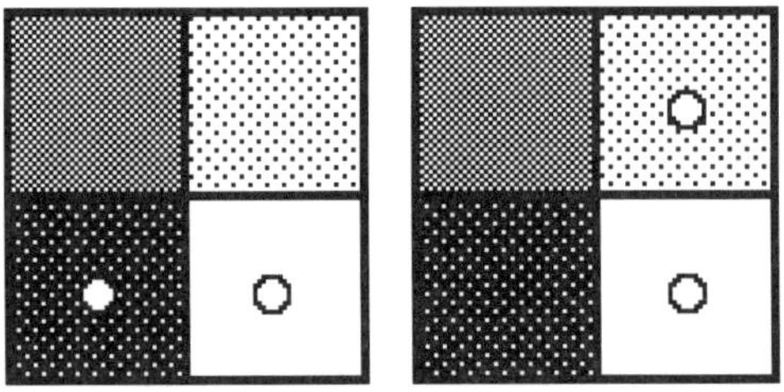

35
or
20 + 10 + 4 + 1

gies for figuring out answers. This was worrisome for I knew simple, one-step multiplication problems were about to become more complex.

Trouble Composing Functions

I asked, "How would you double this [i.e., twice 3 x 35]?" In response, Ron quickly gave the total, "210," arranged checkers, and revealed nothing about the process of multiplication (see Figure 3.6). If students knew what was on the worksheet, they would stick with me and attend to the process. I asked for someone to double the checkers on the Minicomputer. If students understood that 2 groups of 3 groups of 35 was the same as 6 groups of 35, they might see how to label the composition arrow. Arif said he had another way; I welcomed it. I assumed since Ron had already shown the total, Arif would show the number of groups of 35. We all watched as Arif stared at the Minicomputer, moved some checkers around, and added others. After an awkward silence, he said, "I am confused." I asked why. He responded, "Because over here we added three of them and we got 105 and I thought over here we were supposed to add two more of them." I assumed "them" meant 35s. Arif was doing what I had done—addition rather than multiplication. Adding two 35s to the product of 3 x 35, or 105, was not the same as multiplying 3 x 35, or 105, by 2.

I asked, "Does anyone have thoughts for Arif about this?" Bob said, "I know how you can make it a little easier instead of putting all of those checkers on. You could make it easier." I assumed Bob wanted

FIGURE 3.6: The Product of Twice 3 × 35

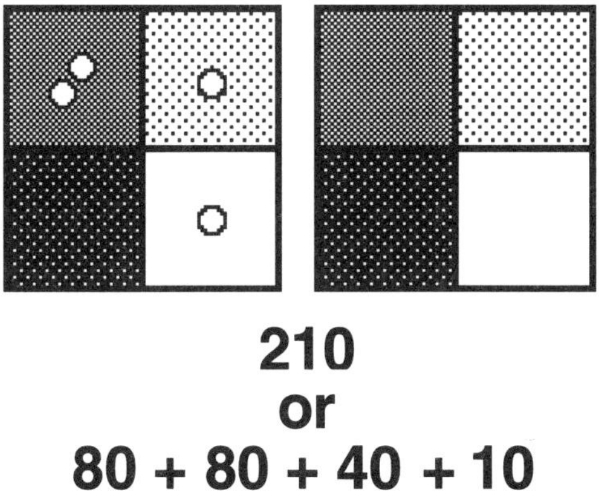

to show the total with the least checkers. We had done enough of that. I cut him off. Least number of checkers might be "easier" in the sense of trying to keep track of the total value of the number on the Minicomputer but Bob's sense of "easier" did not mean illustrating the equal groups in this multiplication problem, which is what was necessary to see to complete the worksheet.

I could show Arif and others the process of composing two multiplicative functions and the correct solution on the Minicomputer. I put aside the teacher's guide and moved beside Arif. As I started to talk, he returned to his desk. I said, "I would like to show you something here." I removed all the checkers Arif had put on the board and replaced only enough to show 35. Then I asked, "What number is this on the Minicomputer? Jennifer?" Jennifer said, "35." Next, I repeated the pattern of 35 on the Minicomputer to show 2 x 35. I said, "Okay. If I want to make this a multiplication problem, what would I say? Using a multiplication sign, how could I make a problem out of this, what could I say? Faruq?" Faruq said, "2 times 35." I repeated what he said and wrote 2 x 35 on the chalkboard. Then, I arranged the checkers again, this time to show 3 times 35 (see Figure 3.7). I asked, "What would I say now with multiplication? Using the multiplication sign, what could I say now? Arif?" He said, "3 times 35." I drew an arrow on the chalkboard and labeled it 3 x. I said, "Now, and this is what some people were having problems with, I want to double this." I added and labeled a second arrow with 2 x (see Figure 3.8). As I did, students chorused, "Ohhhhhhhh," as if they had just seen something in a new way. I said, "Two times what's here," as I pointed to the Minicomputer arranged with checkers illustrating 3 x 35 and the dot for 105 on the arrow road. "How could I do that without moving these checkers and adding

FIGURE 3.7: 3 times 35

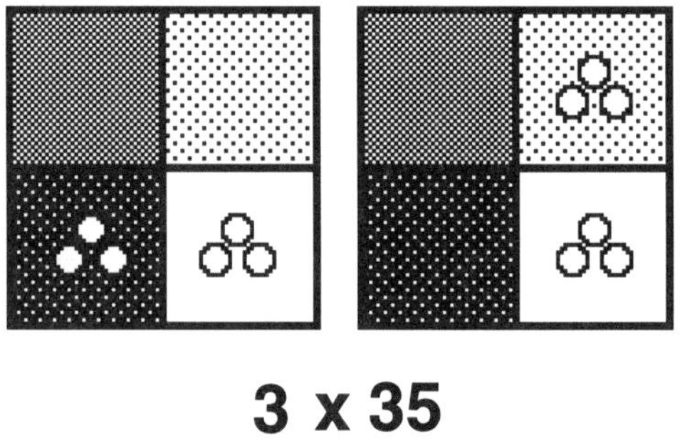

FIGURE 3.8: Doubling 3×35

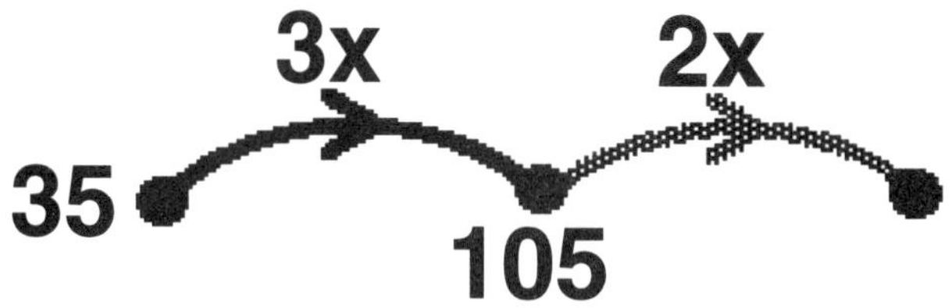

something else to the Minicomputer? Arif?" Arif said, "I remembered now." He stepped forward and repeated the pattern of 3 x 35 on the Minicomputer (see Figure 3.9). As he finished, he said, "I have doubled the whole thing." I asked, "Why did you do it that way? Why does that make sense to you?" He said, "Because you have to double the 105." I labeled the arrows for him (see Figure 3.1). I was content to leave things this way. I wanted to believe that Arif understood. I asked no further questions. If he or others did not understand, I was not sure what else to do. Students were restless and I needed to get them engaged in something. They spent the remaining 15 minutes of class working independently on the worksheet.

FIGURE 3.9: Repeating Patterns of Checkers for 3×35

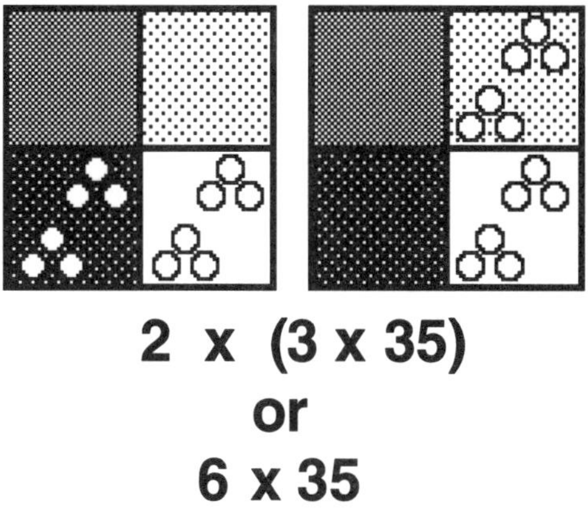

A NOTICED MOMENT: TAKING CONTROL

Lampert observed class that day. As usual, she hurried off after my math class to prepare for her own in the fifth-grade class next door. She handed me her observation notes as she left. We would discuss them later. I was always eager to read Lampert's notes. I still searched her notes for approval, even though I knew her purpose was not evaluation. Lampert wrote:

> Did you get some kind of "bright idea" about how to pull all this together when you said "I want to show you something"? Or were you following the script? It seemed to me as if you were more engaged here, more thinking about the kids and the subject matter and the representation rather than following the manual. It seemed like you saw what they needed in order to get the point. (Lampert observation notes, 09/21/89)

Did I? What moment was she referring to? I was uncertain. None stood out to me. Her observation peaked my curiosity and came at a time when I was searching for anything I might have been doing that resembled the teaching I was aiming to do. Her comment seemed almost like a compliment. Had I finally done something right?

This was a lesson Reineke did not observe but I audio taped. I had the tape with me and decided to replay it. If I located and replayed the moment Lampert noticed, I might understand what she had seen. At home that evening, I located the statement, "I want to show you something," and played and replayed that part of the lesson. The moment Lampert was referring to was when I acted on Arif's confusion representing 2 x (3 x 35) on the Minicomputer. As I listened and considered what had happened, I decided that, indeed, something new had occurred. I made notes in my journal as I listened to the tape.

> I did see what they needed. The point was to see the connection between addition and multiplication. By the time I stepped in, the students had already wandered off the track. They were missing the point and I could see that. I think part of what was happening was that I was clear on the purpose—connection between addition and multiplication—(make use of patterns on the Minicomputer). I also trusted myself. I had the confidence to make a decision about what to do independent of the teacher's guide. (Heaton journal, 09/21/89)

I followed through with something I felt needed to be done. I understood the mathematics children were supposed to be learning and had a way to represent the mathematical idea Arif was trying to understand. In this moment, the teacher's guide (i.e., its way of making use of the Minicomputer to show the process of composing two multiplicative functions) was a meaningful resource I chose to use.

After listening to the tape, I struggled to make a distinction between the teaching I did before and what occurred in this moment.

> Things came together in that moment because I was thinking about the subject, listening to the students and trying to make sense of what they were saying and then I acted. I think this last part is what has been missing until now—the teaching (as a verb, an action) part of teaching for understanding. How do I keep it up? (Heaton journal, 09/21/89)

I moved away from the scripted lesson and made a move that went beyond asking children to explain their thinking. I was connected to the work of teaching in ways that I had not experienced before in mathematics. I was learning I needed to be responsive to the sense particular students made of the mathematics as well as what made sense to me as I considered the question of what to do next in the act of teaching. I had a new feel for teaching. What I had experienced, what Lampert had noticed, was what I was aiming to do. For a moment, I was no longer in the role of a silent bystander listening to children's responses and clinging to the textbook. In my journal I noted that it felt as if momentarily, "I took control. I knew what I was doing" (Heaton journal, 09/21/89). For a fleeting moment, I was teaching.

CHAPTER 4

Learning to Appreciate Teaching as an Improvisational Activity

The moment of interaction with Arif and other students around the problem of doubling 3 x 35, however short-lived, was powerful in that it gave me a new sense for the teaching I wanted to do. Here I re-examine that moment with the aid of an audio tape and transcript to better understand the significance of the moment. What evidence is there, beyond Lampert's observation, that this was a significant moment for me? In what ways was the teaching in this moment different from earlier moments since the school year started? What was changing? What would be required to sustain such moments in teaching for longer periods of time? The questions I ask here are similar to the ones I asked as I listened to the audio tape at the time I was teaching (see Chapter 3). Now, however, the purpose is for studying the broader question of what it would take to learn to teach mathematics for understanding. The immediate need to teach is gone.

LEARNING TO SEE TEACHING AS IMPROVISATION

In the moment Lampert noticed, I was responding directly to Arif, based on what I thought he needed to understand about the mathematics. Yinger's (1988) image of teaching as "responsive and sensitive to context" (p. 90) is helpful in describing the kind of teaching I was aiming to do. In Yinger's discussion, he suggests that the language of "planning, implementation, and reflection" does not capture the essence of this kind of teaching. He prefers the language of "preparation, improvisation, and contemplation" (p. 85), a language more representative of the spontaneous nature of this kind of teaching. Yinger's image of improvisation provides another metaphor parallel to those of learning to navigate a riverboat (see Chapter 2) or learning to play jazz, which I will explore here.

Creating Patterned Responses

Given my knowledge of the math reforms, I knew I needed to change my role in the classroom. In an interview with Reineke before the start of the school year, I described my vision of the teacher's role in relation to students' roles.

> *Reineke:* The next question I was going to ask is if you plan to change your instruction. I think you just answered that to some extent. Is there anything else that you'd like to add to that?
>
> *Heaton:* One thing would be to have them explain their thinking and how they got their answers. I think another change would be for me to take a different role in the classroom, one where the students would do the talking. The students would talk with each other.

As seen in this lesson and the previous one on patterns, to facilitate this shift in roles I had stopped all telling and eliminated any type of evaluation of students' answers. I tried to do nothing but ask questions and remain neutral. In the pattern lesson, I remained silent and uncertain about what students were to supposed to learn. In this lesson, I had a better idea of what children needed to learn to complete the worksheet but remained silent until the moment of interaction with Arif. In both lessons, I accepted all individual answers but was at a loss for how to take individual comments and collectively move forward. I was beginning to feel that math needed to be more than just a time to share ideas. I was thrilled at first to have students doing much of the talking. But as time went on, I had begun to feel as if I ought to be doing something more with responses. I was a *teacher*. I was supposed *to teach*. Letting students share their ideas is only part of the process. How could I show respect for children and their ideas and at the same time fulfill my responsibilities as the teacher who knew things I wanted children to learn? I needed to expand my role beyond silence and it was becoming clearer to me that the CSMP teacher's guide was of limited assistance in helping me figure out what to do next.

As a way of better understanding the moment Lampert noticed, I studied the moments of interaction right before it. What follows is the actual class discussion, transcribed from an audio tape of the lesson. (The suggested teacher's prompt in the CSMP script for this lesson is: "Who can add some checkers so that 3 x 35 is on the Minicomputer?")

Lesson Transcript (09/21/89)

Ms. Heaton: O.K., what if I want to show now, three times? Can someone show me that on the minicomputer? Jamilia?
Jamilia: [Jamilia arranges checkers on the Minicomputer.]
Ms. Heaton: O.K., can you tell me,—us why that is 3 times 35? Can you explain what you did? Can someone help her out? Do you agree with that? Do you disagree? What do you think? Bob?
Bob: I agree because, see, 35 times 3 is just like 3 35s. It is sort of like, it is tripled.
Ms. Heaton: Okay, what do people think about that? Jennifer?
Jennifer: I know how much it is.
Ms. Heaton: And what is it?
Jennifer: 105
Ms. Heaton: How do you know that?
Jennifer: Because I did it in my head again. I did 35 plus 35 plus 35 and then I went 5 plus 5 plus 5 is 15, put down 5 carry the 10. 30 plus 30, plus 30 equals 90 and I would add more 1 more 10 and that's 100.
Ms. Heaton: O.K. and what if I want to show that now on the Minicomputer, 105 times 2? Ron?
Ron: 210.
Ms. Heaton: How do you know that?
Ron: Two times 105 equals, can I show it?
Ms. Heaton: Sure. You can do both. You can show us and tell us.
Ron: 100 plus 100 is 200 and then plus 5 and 5 is 10.
Ms. Heaton: Do you want to show us with this on the Minicomputer a way you can multiply by 2?

It was only a few weeks into the school year but students already knew the routine: I accepted all ways in which they responded to the questions I asked. In retrospect, I am able to see students responding to my request to show 3 x 35, or one-step multiplication problems, in one of 3 ways. I had a way of responding to each.

If Students . . .	I . . .
1) gave me the total or the answer to the multiplication problem,	1) asked, "Can you tell us how you figured it out?"

2) showed the total or the answer to the multiplication problem on the Minicomputer,
3) repeated the pattern of checkers of the number we started with either twice or three times on the Minicomputer, depending on whether a number was multiplied by 2 or 3.

2) asked, as the checkers were placed on the Minicomputer, "Could you tell us what you are doing as you do it?"
3) hovered over their shoulder and helped them to arrange the checkers to create and maintain a pattern. This way took much longer than the others.

The questions in the CSMP teacher's guide, together with ones I inserted about why or how children thought about their answers, served as starting points for improvising a set of patterned responses. I constructed an if–then system: If a student does this, then I do this. While I did not think of these as formulas for improvisation at the time, I can see now that I created patterns of response not found in the teacher's guide. These patterns, however, carried me only so far in response to the question of what to do next.

I could get through the first few moves with a fair amount of certainty about my role. I asked the textbook question, then my own. After that, it was hard to predict what situations might arise and even harder to decide ahead of time what to do next. The situations and decisions about my next moves were getting more complex. At the time, I wrote in my journal (09/21/89), "Somehow I thought following CSMP was going to help me in all of this. Now, I am beginning to question what it means to follow a book in this kind of teaching." I was beginning to see that it was necessary to respond to the question of what to do next in the moment. Sometimes the guide might help. Other times not. What I needed to learn was how to respond and be responsive to students in the act of teaching beyond these initial interactions. Sudnow (1978) writes of learning a similar kind of moment-to-moment responsiveness in the playing of improvisational jazz.

> For a long while, I guided my hands through the terrain of the keyboard by moving my fingers along the various routes and scales I had conceived . . . they were part of a way of proceeding other than what I do now. I am not using pathways to make up melodies. Now I find places to go in the course of going to them, each particular next place at a time, doing improvisation. (p. xii)

To do this, I needed to continue to move away from the script and do more complex improvisation.

Deciding What to Do Next

What happened in my interaction with Arif? In what ways was it like the patterned responses? In what ways was it different? The first student to respond gave the total, 210, when I asked how to double 3 x 35. The offering of a total was similar to students' earlier responses when asked the same question. Rather than pursue how the total was figured with the student who offered it, which was part of my predictable routine, I called on Arif, who said he had another way. With empathy for Arif's confusion after he tried to show his way with checkers, I asked if he could explain why he was feeling confused. I tried to push his thinking with a question—a question specific to this situation—that I hoped might lead him to see what I thought he needed to learn. This was a different move from those I had done in the past. I asked, "Does that sign tell you to add, what are you doing?" I was asking a question for the purpose of helping him see something new, not to merely share his ideas. Examining this question from my current perspective, it seems I assumed Arif's difficulty was in his literal understanding of the multiplication sign. In hindsight, the difficulty probably had more to do with the limits of his understanding of the relationship between addition and multiplication than with misreading the multiplication sign. Perhaps a better question would have been, "What was being doubled?" The answer to that is what Arif needed to see.

I continued asking if anyone had ideas to help Arif. Asking how others saw the problem was not a move away from Arif, as it had been earlier, for example, in my move from Ron to Arif. Calling on someone else was a deliberate strategy to help Arif see what he needed. I called on Bob. As it turned out, Bob's response of how to use the least number of checkers to represent the total was not going to help with Arif's confusion. Therefore, in a move quite unlike what I had been doing earlier in this lesson and in the 3 weeks since school began, I interrupted Bob and said, "I want to show you something."

As I look back on it now, I find it ironic that in this moment, the first time I felt as if I was teaching, I was telling. I had consciously replaced declarative statements with countless questions and listened to students' ideas. I felt frustrated that mathematically we went nowhere. Perhaps showing or telling did have a place in this teaching. I could decide when and why to do it. The telling I did in this situation was a move in response to a child's understanding. This is quite different from the kind of telling I did in my past practice, independent of students' understanding. The teaching standards (NCTM, 1991) describe the teacher's role in classroom discourse and the place of telling.

> Beyond asking clarifying or provocative questions, teachers should also, at times, provide information and lead students. Decisions about when to let students struggle to make sense of an idea or a problem without direct teacher input, when to ask leading questions, and when to tell students something directly are crucial to orchestrating productive mathematical discourse in the classroom. (p. 36)

This moment of telling marked my entrance into the "conversation of practice" (Yinger, 1988, p. 74).

THE SIGNIFICANCE OF THE MOMENT: MOVING FROM ADDITION TO MULTIPLICATION

My analysis of dealing with mathematical ideas underlying pattern and function identification in Chapter 2 grew out of my efforts to hear students. Here, I do a similar exploration of the mathematical ideas embedded in a task, but for a somewhat different purpose. In this instance, I "heard" Arif's confusion and had one way to respond. Would I have been better prepared to respond to Arif's confusion in multiple ways if I had a deeper appreciation for the mathematical ideas in this situation? In both instances, children's responses become sites for my own study of mathematical ideas. This kind of task analysis for the purpose of trying to understand the cognitive demands on a teacher complements much of the task analysis research in mathematics education (e.g., Hiebert & Wearne, 1992) done for the purpose of understanding the cognitive demands placed on children.

The composition of functions in the context of multiplication pushes at an area of fundamental mathematics, namely, the move from additive to multiplicative structures. Leinhardt, Zaslavsky, and Stein (1990) describe this transition as "one of the critical moments in early mathematics" that are opportunities for "powerful learning" with two interesting features: "They are often unmarked in the 'normal' course of teaching; on the other hand, they are fundamental to other more sophisticated parts of mathematics" (p. 2). What 2 x (3 x 35) represents is a move from an additive world "where successive elements have a constant (additive) difference" to a multiplicative world, "where successive elements have a constant (multiplicative) ratio (Smith & Confrey, 1994, p. 338).

True to the pattern Leinhardt, Zaslavsky, and Stein (1990) found in most other math curricula, the mathematical significance of the leap from one territory to another in the context of this problem goes unmarked in the CSMP teacher's guide. Perhaps I could have identified these critical moments within the CSMP curriculum if I had a picture of the whole curriculum, across a year as well as relative to other grade levels. This, however, is not an understanding I had at the time I was teaching.

Moving from the additive world to multiplicative structures is a complex conceptual leap for students to make (Harel & Confrey, 1994; Vergnaud, 1988). One fundamental problem is that students bring many experiences with addition when they make their way into the multiplicative world. An understanding of multiplication often is built on an understanding of addition. It is common for students to make connections between addition and multiplication or to think of multiplication as repeated addition. For example, students tend to think of a problem like 3 x 35 in additive terms—adding 35 three times—rather than as multiplying the unit of quantity (Behr, Harel, Post, & Lesh, 1994), 35, by three. Repeated addition produces a solution but offers a limited view of the meaning of multiplication.

Composing the functions, 3 x followed by 2 x, put students in the multiplicative world. They immediately returned to the additive world, a place of comfort, given the focus on additive structures in earlier grades, to work it. I did the same when I first worked the problem. Usually, multiplication as repeated addition works. For example, 3 x 35 is the same as 35 + 35 + 35. But the relationship between addition and multiplication becomes more complicated when you try to multiply (3 x 35) by 2. To Arif, from an additive perspective, it looked as if he needed to add two 35s to three 35s. In response to the question why he was adding two 35s he said, "Because over here we added three of them and we got 105 and I thought over here we were supposed to add two more of them." There are multiple incorrect but predictable ways someone with a limited view of multiplication might try to symbolically represent this problem (see Figure 4.1).

What Arif and I did not understand, at first, is that the composition of functions brings out the complexity and difficulty of multiplication. Consider the problem 2 x (3 x 35) in terms of inputs and outputs. If I begin with 35 as the input, apply times three to this, and consider multiplication as repeated addition, I get one group of 35 plus another group of 35 plus another group of 35. These three groups of 35 (3 x 35) or (35 + 35 + 35) become the new input to which I apply times two. This is key. The input or unit changes from 35 to three 35s. The solution should be two sets of three 35s or six 35s rather than two more 35s added to a set of three groups of 35. That the input or unit changes from 35 to (35 + 35 + 35) is difficult to understand (see Figure 4.2).

FIGURE 4.1: Predictable But Incorrect Ways to Represent 2 × (3 × 35)

$$(35 + 35 + 35) + 35 + 35$$

or

$$(5 \times 35)$$

or

$$(3 \times 35) + (2 \times 35)$$

or

$$(105) + 35 + 35$$

Adding two units of the quantity, 35, to a set of three 35s is very different from duplicating the set of three 35s. Hiebert and Behr (1988) describe the significance of multiplicative change.

> It is not a trivial shift, because it represents a change in what counts as a number. A group or composite . . . now can count as a unit, as one. A change in the nature of the unit is a change in the most basic entity of arithmetic. (p. 2)

At the time, I did not have a clear understanding of the symbolic relationship between addition and multiplication represented by the possible interpretations of the problem, nor was I as clear about the mathematical complexity of a change of units. I was able to set up the

FIGURE 4.2: The Input Changes from 35 to 35 + 35 + 35

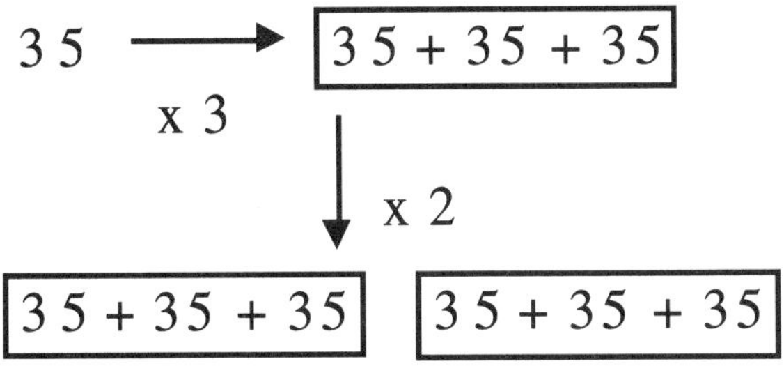

Minicomputer and illustrate the numbers of groups, but I did not have multiple ways to consider the symbolic representation of what was happening. There was one alternative symbolic representation for multiplication offered in the teacher's guide. It came in the context of the following teacher question.

> *T*: What is 3 x 35? What is 35 + 35 + 35?

There was no discussion about how these two symbolic representations, 3 x 35 and 35 + 35 + 35, are related, or the effects on symbolic representation when one composes functions. What I lacked at the time was a knowledge of representations, "analogies, illustrations, examples, explanations, demonstrations, the ways of representing and formulating the subject to make it comprehensible to others" (Shulman, 1986, p. 9). The Minicomputer was a representation I had at my disposal, but my understanding of the significance of the mathematical ideas it represented was limited by the information or lack of it offered within the teacher's guide. What I subsequently have come to understand about the significance of composing these two functions came out of my own informal study of the mathematics through reading and talking with others about the topic. Were I to teach this lesson again, I would have other ways of symbolically representing the composition of these two functions. Improvisational musicians learn and expand their own repertoires in a similar manner.

> The important overall considerations are to permit oneself the opportunity of all the possibilities you can envisage . . . and to be continually on the lookout (by listening to yourself and your co-improvisers, by hearing other improvisers perform) for new inputs. (Dean, 1989, p. 111).

LEARNING TO PREPARE FOR IMPROVISATION

I found myself *in* teaching in ways I had not experienced before. For a moment I felt what it was like to improvise, to be responsive, beyond the first few moves, to students' understanding and the mathematics I was aiming to teach. What is that state of being I am learning to be in as a part of teaching? What had Lampert noticed? This is where Sudnow's (1978) description of learning to play improvisational jazz is useful. He and his hands must learn to be "singingly present" (p. 90) with his fingers in the terrain—seeing, hearing, feeling, choosing pathways.

One of the first steps in preparing to choose a path is learning something about the territory and possible pathways through it. I now see the teacher's guide as a path through the terrain. Initially, I saw the teacher's guide in mathematics as the terrain itself. Viewing the teacher's guide as just one path opens up the possibility that there may be other paths to follow. It makes following the teacher's guide a choice, based on the appropriateness of the exigencies of the moment. This is similar to the action of telling—not something to be thoughtlessly used or abandoned but something I can choose to integrate purposefully into my practice.

The same idea of choice can be extended to tools, like the Minicomputer, that can help teachers move about in the terrain, along different paths. The Minicomputer is a tool or a path, a figure in the terrain, not the terrain. The purpose is not to teach the Minicomputer, but to use this tool to help see something that might otherwise go unnoticed in the terrain. I always run the risk that what enables me to see might not be what enables someone else. That is why I need a repertoire of tools or pathways for helping others to see. Learning what pathways are possible and learning how to decide which path to take is part of the work entailed in learning to improvise.

What can I do to prepare myself to improvise? Leonard Bernstein (Mehegan, 1959) recognized both the wish and the impossibility of ever being able to write down in a textbook all the knowledge needed to improvise music.

> There has long been a need for a sharp, clear, wise textbook which would once and for all codify and delineate that elusive procedure known as jazz improvisation. Of course, no improvisation can ever be explained down to its roots; therein lies the mystery and joy of spontaneous creation. And any improvisation will vary greatly in proportion to talent, mood, colleagues, and endless personal factors. (p. 6)

A solution in mathematics might be to construct a textbook that can serve as a guide, rather than a script, for improvisation. This textbook needs to treat teaching as an activity that links children's understandings and fundamental mathematical ideas. The teacher needs to have information about possible links as well as general understandings about how children might make sense of mathematical ideas and the significance of these ideas from a disciplinary perspective. This kind of information could be compiled in a teacher's guide, created by authorities on particular mathematical topics. It is the kind of information a teacher acquires informally over time through experiences teaching children mathematics. Mack (1970) offers the following advice for keeping track of this informal knowledge:

> Don't try to "learn" improvisations. Once you've decided on an approach, try to vary the key, the tempo, the mood, the meter, the register. Try to use your wits and don't rely on rote or repetition. On the other hand, you may find it useful to keep a notebook of good ideas—material that serves well for certain purposes. (p.1)

The notebook I kept is my journal. Several days after this lesson, I noted in it that I was "writing my plans differently—making decisions." When Lampert read through my journal, next to this comment she wrote, "Noting the difference in how you plan seems crucial." Why? Yinger (1988) argues that if we draw an analogy between teaching and improvisation, then we need to consider planning as preparation.

> Preparation acknowledges our limited ability to predict and the constructive nature of life. Preparation expects diversity, surprise, the random, and the wild. To prepare is to get ready, to become equipped, and to become receptive. The focus of preparation is on oneself, not on a framework to constrain possibility. In a sense, preparation enlarges the future. (p. 88)

It seems that Lampert was already anticipating changes in the nature of my planning given the nature of the changes happening in my teaching (see Heaton, 1991). That I would indicate I was "making decisions" while planning seems further evidence I was thinking differently about what I needed to do to prepare. Preparation for improvising jazz music involves "prehearing," as Mehegan (1959) writes.

> Prehearing means a memorized hearing—heard in anticipation of the moment of playing. This is the ideal we all seek and is the reason why fine jazz playing is a challenge both to play and appreciate. (p. 201)

My next challenge is to learn to anticipate these moments and sustain the feel of improvisation for longer than a single moment.

CHAPTER 5

Bendable Rulers and Other Moments of Improvisation

I had begun to get the feel for what it meant to improvise in teaching. What was intended by CSMP to be a one-day lesson to make labels for soup cans in the Geometry strand evolved into five lessons in a row in mid-October, each one building on the previous one. This lesson summary appeared in the CSMP teacher's guide.

Capsule Lesson Summary

> Make labels for cans. Discuss how size problems might be reduced by measuring to the nearest millimeter instead of to the nearest centimeter. (McREL, 1986, p. 6)

Improvisation played a role in the creation of these lessons and how they unfolded. I find myself connected in important ways to students' interactions. We are learning to improvise together.

RECTANGLES

To start the lesson, I stood at the front of the room with a soup can in my hands. "What shape do you think the label will be when I pull it off the can?" I asked. Ron's arm immediately shot up in the air. His was the only hand raised. I nodded to him and he proclaimed with great certainty, "A rectangle." I asked him how he knew. His personal experience with labels surprised me. "My mom collects soup can labels. She saves them down flat." Ron explained, "If you stretch them out, the shape of the label is a rectangle."

I followed up Ron's response with a question that had become part of my improvised responses to whatever someone first said. I asked, "What do other people think?" Everyone agreed. Considering Ron's evidence, how could anyone disagree? I wondered how others would have answered the question without Ron's experience to draw on. I never expected the answer about the shape of the label to come so quickly.

I followed up with another question not in the teacher's guide, "What makes something a rectangle?" By fourth grade, most students were able to identify shapes as rectangles. Identifying a shape as a rectangle was one thing. Articulating the properties of a rectangle was quite another. Several students, including John, raised their hands. He was shy and timid so whenever I saw his hand raised, I called on him. He said, "If two ends are the same size, like if two ends are little and two ends are littler than the other two ends." This seemed like the beginning of a definition from which one could begin to infer properties of rectangles (i.e., opposite sides are equal). He struggled for language. I hoped others could offer words that would help John articulate what he meant.

> *Ms. Heaton:* O.K., what do people think about John's idea? So, two ends are littler than the other two ends. Are there other things that make something a rectangle or do you have other comments about John's idea? Luke?
>
> *Luke:* I challenge. I think like if two ends are littler than the other two ends, then it would be going down like a triangle. It would be, it just wouldn't be a rectangle.

Somewhat frustrated, John asked, "Can I show him on the board?" His cheeks were flushed and he was speechless. I did not want him to withdraw from the discussion and give up. That was his usual way of coping with disagreement. He drew a rectangle. "This is what I mean. These two ends are little and these two ends are long," he explained (see Figure 5.1). Rising in his chair to see the board, Luke said, "Oh. That's not what you said." With a slightly pained look on his face, John softly replied, "Well, I tried to say it."

In other situations, I had seen Luke try to understand something from another's perspective so I assumed that he was genuinely puzzled by John's definition. I did not want John to drop out of this exchange. I said, "John, how could you make it clearer to Luke what you meant?"

FIGURE 5.1: John's Rectangle

John chose several new words and spoke again, "Two of the ends are shorter and two of the ends are longer." It was not clear whether this made more sense to Luke. I noticed David kneeling on his chair, his hand waving in the air. I invited him to share his thoughts. David said, "Can I show something up on the board? I disagree with John when he said that because, like, see, like this, if you have five ends and these two ends are longer, it is not in the shape of a rectangle" (see Figure 5.2).

He had a good point. This shape did fit John's definition but definitely was not a rectangle. I was concerned, however, about David's tone of voice. It hinted at competition rather than cooperation. In his quiet way, John was a leader in this class. While more vocal, David was also a leader. Competitive interactions between several other pairs of students had prompted me to notice the distinction between disagreeing with someone for the sake of disagreeing with the *person* and disagreeing with someone because of disagreement with their *ideas*. I tended to step in and take the lead when I thought it was the former and remain quiet during the latter. It was never easy for me to decide which was which. I often recognized what seemed like pickiness after it had gone too far. I held back here to see if I could tell which this was.

John looked at David's drawing and said, "Well, you'd need four." David ran his finger around the sides of the figure he drew and counted, "One, two, three, four, five." John revised his definition. "There is two short ends and two long ends and there is not five ends. There is four ends." David took an eraser, removed a fifth side and said, "There, that has four ends."

Changing the Dynamic

Was David really helping John revise and construct a definition of a rectangle or was he picking on him and trying to make him look foolish? As a teacher, it was a hard call. David's questions were forcing John to be more explicit about the assumptions embedded in his defini-

FIGURE 5.2: David's Interpretation of John's Work

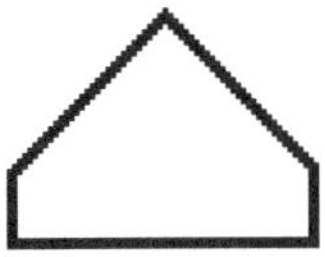

tion, but at what cost? How was John going to feel when this was over? In response to David's drawing, John asked, "Can you connect it?" To this David responded, "It is connected," and ran his finger around the sides.

On the one hand, I sensed David did understand what John said and was finding legitimate holes in his definition. This was a reasonable way for an individual to help John revise his ideas and for the group to construct some shared definition of a rectangle. On the other hand, I felt uneasy about the sharpness in David's voice and redness in John's face. Some students squirmed in their seats and glanced from the two boys at the chalkboard to me at the side of the room and then back to the boys at the front. I read their movements as a request for me to do something.

I moved to the front of the room and asked, "Can we think of a way to talk about a rectangle that describes a shape that looks like this?" (see Figure 5.1). "John has given us a good start. Two ends are short and two ends are long and there are four ends. How else could we, what could we do to add to that description to make it clearer that we are talking about something like this?" I pointed to John's rectangle. David and John returned to their seats. The group relaxed. The tension in the air eased. It was now a group task to use John's ideas to construct a definition of a rectangle.

After Class

In my journal, I reported on a conversation I had with the classroom teacher immediately after class. She said to me, "After this class, I don't care if you spend 2 weeks on the can [i.e., making labels]." This was an important statement. While I took responsibility for teaching mathematics, she took overall responsibility and front-line accountability for what children were learning in her classroom. We both worried about the slow pace at which I was moving through the CSMP curriculum. Because of moves like this, I was far behind according to CSMP's master schedule. But maybe I needed to rethink the meaning of moving ahead. Perhaps the number of CSMP lessons done was not the way to be thinking about covering the curriculum. For example, making labels for cans was the driving goal when I started this lesson, but I was beginning to think that might not be the point. This was an example of a rich activity with the potential for leading in many mathematically interesting directions. I decided to spend a few days playing around with whatever came up. This was a whole new way for me to think about a math curriculum. On the one hand, the structured freedom to move as I pleased made me a bit nervous. On the other hand, the discussion of rectangles was nothing I planned, yet it created my longest feel for this kind of teaching.

STRINGS AND CANS

Unbeknownst to the students, I began the next math class with a long piece of string in my pocket and plans in my head for using it to measure the circumference of a can. Here were the directions as they appeared in the CSMP teacher's guide.

> Measure to the nearest centimeter the circumference of your can and its height. Use a metric tape measure, or cut pieces of string in the appropriate lengths and then measure the string. Label the measurements of your can. (McREL, 1986, p. 8)

I kept the string in my pocket until I saw how someone measured the circumference of the can. I wanted students to see the need for an alternative method before I provided one.

Arif demonstrated a method of measuring a can. All eyes were glued on him as he stood before the group rolling the can along his ruler. The measuring of a round object with a straight edge was an awkward process to watch and even more awkward to do. The can slipped, the ruler slid and shook, fingers got in the way, eyes could not read numbers. Arif started, stopped, and began to measure the can several times. He knelt on the floor at the front of the room, eye level with the can that rested on top of an empty desk. One hand held the ruler straight, parallel to the top of the desk, perpendicular to and in front of the can. The other hand reached behind the ruler and rotated the can along the edge of the ruler. He slowly rotated the can one time as he marked the start of the rotation on the side of the can and tried to watch as the number of centimeters increased. When the can rotated back to where it started, Arif announced, "About 22 centimeters." As he returned to his seat, I recorded Arif's finding under the word "circumference" on the chalkboard and noted his name next to it. His noble but cumbersome attempt set a perfect stage for where I wanted to move next. I fingered the string in my pocket.

The students decided, after witnessing the problems Arif faced with the ruler, that an alternative means, preferably something that would bend around the can, would be useful. Arif concurred. I pulled the string from my pocket and offered it as a means for measuring the circumference. Wu Lee volunteered to demonstrate a way to use the string. All eyes were fixed on her as she held the ends of the string and wrapped it around the middle of the can. The string was longer than the circumference of the can. With intense concentration, she used the fingers of one hand to mark the length of string she needed. As she pulled the string from the can, she tried to keep her fingers positioned in the same place. I noticed her fingers slip. She glanced at me over the top of her glasses and replaced her fingers at about the same spot. She laid the length of string between her fingers along the edge of her ruler and announced, "26 centimeters." As I noted this on the chalkboard along with her name, many hands rose in the air. Others wanted a turn at measuring the can with a string.

Luke disclosed concern for the tension of the string. "I think it might work to place the string at the bottom of the can, wrap it around, and then make sure it is nice and tight." I asked, "Why does it need to be tight?" Luke reasoned, "Because if it is loose, it could add a few more centimeters than what it really is." Luke tried his method. Placing the string around the bottom of the can allowed him to use the desk to steady the string. His fingers marked the spot and he laid the string on the ruler and pulled it tight. "Twenty-one centimeters," he announced. As I put his name and measurement on the board, many hands shot up into the air.

I was surprised to see Faruq's hand. Faruq never volunteered and I was uncertain how to draw him in. The room fell silent as he stepped forward. Everyone seemed to recognize how exceptional this moment was. He carefully measured the can's circumference. He bent to his knees as Arif did, pulled the string not quite as tight as Luke, and was careful not to let his fingers slip nearly as much as Wu Lee's. Faruq laid the string along the ruler and whispered, "23 centimeters." I added his name and measurement to the growing list on the board. As Faruq returned to his seat, I noticed that he glanced several times over his shoulder at the chalkboard. This was probably the first time his name had been attached to an idea in math class. I had never seen him more confident. I felt awful. I had been thinking that learning math for understanding was just too hard for him. It had taken until mid-October for me to see that he had something to contribute.

I quickly called on Jennifer who, it turned out, had been thinking about the finger slippage problem. She had noticed that centimeters appeared to get lost or found somewhere in the process between wrapping the string around the can and placing it along the edge of the ruler. She inquired, "Could I cut the string?" This was a new idea for all of us. I asked her to demonstrate. She fetched a pair of scissors. Carefully, like the students before her, she wrapped the string around the can. This time, however, she snipped the string at the point where it made its way around the can. Jennifer measured the cut piece of string along the edge of a ruler and declared, "22½ centimeters."

Pacing

It was now 20 minutes into the lesson. Some students were getting restless, while others appeared listless. The measuring of a single can had gone on way too long. It had held the attention of five students who had had a chance to measure, but what about the others? I decided that I needed to quickly get a can and string into everyone's hands. Out of the corner of my eye I saw Sipho's hand raised. I wondered what to do. I began the year with the problem of getting a discussion going. Now, I found myself with the problem of how to end one.

I had particular concerns about Sipho. His way of contributing had been bothering me. Perhaps it was more accurate to say that what bothered me was the way I had been feeling when Sipho had something to contribute. I hated to admit that at times I felt as if I did not want to call on him. But I did. From my perspective, he almost never gave a concise answer. His were always long, detailed, rambling, and hard to follow. If I was looking for a way to end a discussion, calling on Sipho would not bring closure. Often, because his ideas did not necessarily follow on those that had come before, or it was not apparent to me that they did, I questioned whether he had been listening. I knew I was going to need to listen carefully for a long time if I did decide to call on him. Did I have the patience? Could I spare the time? This part of the lesson had already gone on too long. This was reason enough to move on. It was also reason to take a few more minutes and hear what Sipho had to say. "O.K., Sipho, this is the last comment before we all get cans. What are you thinking?"

Sipho began, "I wanted to say that they each got different answers. I notice that they each got different answers and they used the same string. I am wondering why they got different answers if they measured the same can." He had made a keen observation. I scolded myself for my reluctance to let him participate. The accuracy of measurement was an important idea and his observation was insightful. I suspected many people tuned out of this activity long ago so I repeated what Sipho said and asked what others thought about his observation. Ron interpreted Sipho's observation as a question about why it was that the circumference of each of the cans would have a different measurement and attributed it to differences among manufacturing companies. Mike disagreed.

This was not how he understood Sipho's question. He pointed to the chalkboard and paraphrased what he saw, "Jennifer got 22½, Faruq got 23, Luke got 21, Wu Lee got 26, and Arif got 22. They got all different answers for just this one little can." Students offered their own reasons why measurements were inconsistent, and someone suggested they measure their own cans more than once just to be certain of the size. Sipho's comment brought new life to an activity for which many had lost interest.

After Class

In an interview with Reineke later that day, I recounted what occurred just before I called on Sipho.

> There were kids that were up out of their desks. I had other kids, like Jennifer, who were practically asleep. I wanted to move it and get cans into all of their hands. And this is why . . . I hesitated and almost did not call on Sipho for that reason . . . I was ready to bulldoze ahead. If I had, I would have missed that question . . . I think it is a good question . . . why we got all different answers when different people have been measuring the same can with the same string. . . . You know what else I found interesting about Sipho's question? Did you notice that they talked to each other and did not go through me during that part of today's discussion?

Sipho asked a good question from a mathematical perspective. It gave others something interesting to talk about. It certainly gave me something to consider. How many times had I not called on him when he had something to contribute? How many other students was I not seeing? Faruq was showing me all students could learn. Sipho was showing me all students could teach.

The Next Day: A Bendable Ruler

Not until Sipho stopped me on the way into class the next day did I realize he took home with him worries about the discrepancies in measurement he noticed the day before. With his face beaming, he lunged out of his seat when he saw me, dashed across the room, and said, "Ms. Heaton, I bet you can't guess what I brought with me today." I could not guess nor was I sure that I wanted to. There was another lesson going on with the classroom teacher and I thought he should pay closer attention to that instead of talking to me. For the second time in 2 days I was confronted with my feelings about Sipho.

According to the rules, he was supposed to be sitting down and participating in whatever the group was doing. I recalled his contribution of yesterday, saw the excitement on his face, and suppressed the urge to send him back to his seat. I whispered, "Let's move over here," and shuffled us over as far to the side of the room as we could get. I turned to face him, crouched so I was at his eye level, and noticed that he had one hand behind his back.

The hand behind Sipho's back brought to mind the assortment of trinkets that he had at school almost every day. He defended them as falling into the school supply category whenever I objected to their presence on the top of his desk. For example, he owned erasers that looked like circus animals, pens that sparkled like magic wands, pencil sharpeners that resembled miniature automobiles, and pencils that balanced tiny cartoon characters on the eraser end. Anytime I suggested he put his toys away because they appeared to me to be distractions, he reminded me of their role in schoolwork and immediately put them to their intended use. While my history with Sipho made me a bit skeptical about what occupied the hand behind his back that day, the situation seemed different. In his interactions with me, Sipho usually made an effort to conceal rather than reveal his treasures.

I was also a bit hesitant to prolong a conversation with him. In just a few minutes I was supposed to start teaching math. But Sipho looked as if he would burst if he could not tell me what he brought. It was clear to me that whatever he had was very important to him and he thought it was going to be to me, too. "No, Sipho," I said, "I can't guess what you brought, why don't you just tell me." Sipho could hardly contain his enthusiasm. He was no longer whispering. "Well, remember how we were measuring cans yesterday and we were doing it with strings and rulers and everybody was getting different measurements because it was hard trying to use the string. Well, I was talking to my dad and he has this special kind of ruler. I asked and he said I could bring it today. I think it's going to help us." Taking his hand from behind his back, he held out a shiny gray green metal ruler for me to admire. "See what it can do," he said as he bent it into a semicircle. Sipho was right. This was no ordinary straight edge. It was a bendable ruler.

I immediately altered my plans. I decided Sipho would begin by showing everyone this new tool and demonstrate how it would be useful in measuring a can. Then, we would discuss students' measurements of their cans from the day before. I realized I rarely gave Sipho and his ideas this sort of attention. He was never the first to be called on and he was lucky to be the last. Somehow, he and I had started the year off on the wrong foot. I was learning to see him as a resource for constructing curriculum rather than as an obstacle to covering it.

DIMENSIONS

By the end of the next class period, all students had figured out how to measure cans with strings and had done so several times. We had discussed their measurements. The time had come to transfer measurements of each can into dimensions for making labels out of construction paper. The CSMP teacher's guide directed:

> Ask the students to draw a rectangle on a slip of paper and to record the measurements of their cans near the sides of the rectangles. (McREL, 1986, p. 8)

There was no indication in the teacher's guide that following this part of the directions might cause some confusion. Representing height and circumference of the can turned out to be a difficult task for many students and more conceptually complex than either the teacher's guide or I expected.

Rather than just have students go off on their own and record their measurements as directed by the teacher's guide, I had a hunch there might be something we could discuss about these directions. I started the next phase of the label-making process by drawing a rectangle on the board. I told students the rectangle represented a label and they needed to take the dimensions of their cans and apply them to the label. Recording the measurement of these dimensions on this rectangle was an intermediate step I created. I asked if someone would record the height of the can on the rectangle I had drawn on the board. Bob volunteered and went to the chalkboard. We all watched as he stood at the chalkboard and looked puzzled. He could not figure out where to record the height of the can on the rectangle. He took a piece of chalk and added a few lines to the rectangle to make something that looked like this (see Figure 5.3). He said, "I made a 3-D picture of a rectangle

FIGURE 5.3: Bob's 3-D Rectangle

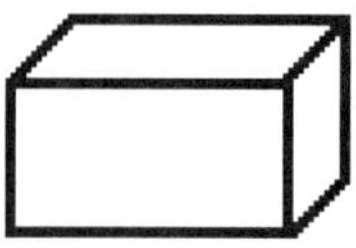

so you can see where the height is . . . because it looks more realistic than just the rectangle," as he pointed to and labeled the height of what he had just drawn. "11 centimeters," he announced.

I heard someone say, "Oh, 3-D, that is neat." I was not sure I thought it was so neat. Thinking about the label as something that looked like what Bob drew was not going to be too helpful, but students seemed interested in the idea of three dimensions. What should I do? I could understand Bob's confusion, although the possibility of this interpretation was nothing I had considered before class. A can has a height, while the rectangle I drew has a length and width. I had asked him to record his can's height.

I was curious what students understood about dimensions and decided I would lead us away from making labels for a moment. I asked, "What do you mean by 3-D?" Ron responded, "Three dimensions." I pushed, "What do you mean by three dimensions?" As I asked, I wondered how I would have responded to the question. Ron did not hesitate, "The first dimension is just a line in space." While Ron talked, the bell rang that marked the end of math and start of lunch. I signaled for the class to remain quiet. I had not realized it was so close to lunch when I started us in this new direction. Ron continued, "The second is depth. It is how we can be able to pick up a pencil. Without it, let's say our pencil is right there, your hand would go right through it. We wouldn't be able to pick it up. And the third dimension is . . . " Inside the classroom, students were restless and hungry. Outside, others were talking on their way to the lunchroom. All of this made it difficult to hear Ron. He continued to talk through the noise, "They are also working on a fourth dimension, which is time, I think."

Before I dismissed students for lunch, I announced, perhaps a bit too hastily, that we would continue this talk of dimensions during the next math class. Class often ended the way this one did, at the sound of the bell, in the midst of a conversation. Often I said we would continue what we were doing but we did not, at least not immediately. The talk of dimensions seemed to have sparked quite an interest among students and I was impressed by Ron's competent definition of the dimensions. On these grounds alone, I decided it was worth spending more time on it the next day.

What Is a Dimension Anyway?

The following day, I asked Bob to draw the "3-D" picture he had made during the previous math class (see Figure 5.3). I returned to Ron and asked him to tell us, again, how he understood dimensions. I thought starting with his definition would be a good place to begin.

Ron: 3-D means three dimensional, that's just a short name for it. And a couple of the other dimensions are [*pause*]. Can I go up to the board? Well, the second dimension Bob already has up there. But the first, he doesn't.

Ms. Heaton: Where is the second dimension?

Ron: The one that Bob just drew.

Bob: No, that is third dimensional.

Other students join Bob: That's third, Ron.

Ms. Heaton: What are you thinking about, do you want to tell us more?

Ron: The first dimension is just a line through space. The second dimension is depth. If you are just flying through space and you just keep on trying to grab a pencil it would, your hand would just go right through it so it has to have depth.

Bob interrupted Ron, again, and started to talk. I told Bob to let Ron talk and when Ron was done he was more than welcome to comment on what had been said. Bob was annoyed. Ron continued:

> See, the second dimension is depth. If this was just a line through space it wouldn't have depth. Depth means how deep it is. But if we add depth here, even paper has a depth of about a oneth of a centimeter, less than a millimeter. Everything has a depth if we just look . . . without it we could walk through walls. We couldn't build houses.

The more Ron talked, the harder it became for me to follow what he was saying. Maybe his understanding of dimensions was not as sophisticated as I had assumed. Maybe it would help if we focused on one dimension at a time.

Ms. Heaton: Could you tell me again, what you are thinking when you think of the first dimension? What are you thinking about?

Ron: The first dimension is just a line through space.

Ms. Heaton: And the second dimension?

Ron: Depth.

Ms. Heaton: And the third dimension?

Ron: I am not sure of that.

Ms. Heaton: Are there other people that want to comment on these dimensions? David, what are you thinking?

David: Can I go up there? I want to challenge Ron on what he

FIGURE 5.4: Ron's Drawing to Show the First Dimension

said. He said that this is from the second dimension. This (see Figure 5.3) is the third dimension.

Ms. Heaton: Can you explain?

David: I don't really know what the third dimension is I just, I think there, the second dimension looks almost like this and Ron might have got them mixed up or I don't know. But I do know this is three dimensional because I used to watch a T.V. show and the guy, he always talked while he drew and he would draw a 3-D square and he would do something like this.

Ms. Heaton: What do other people think? Jamilia?

Jamilia: I don't know what Ron said.

Ms. Heaton: Do you want to ask him a question?

Jamilia: I just don't understand what you were saying.

Ron: Can I go to the board? The first dimension is this line through space. It looks like that (see Figure 5.4). The second dimension is depth (see Figure 5.5).

Ms. Heaton: And how does that show depth?

Ron: You know how like the depth of, the depth of air, air doesn't have depth. Well it does but not the depth that I mean. What I am trying to say is that the third dimension is kind of like the power to pick things up. This drawing is the second dimension because you can't reach in there and grab it and pull it out . . . . It may look like the third dimension but it is not.

FIGURE 5.5: Ron's Drawing to Show the Second Dimension

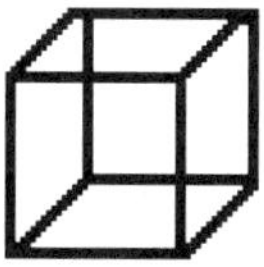

The discussion continued. A handful of other people joined in. There was a struggle with the question of dimensions and a debate about the second and third dimensions.

At times like these I wondered what students were thinking who were not raising their hands. Were they feeling lost? Some of them might have been daydreaming but others could have been really trying to make sense of the ideas of those who were talking. I was never quite sure. One difficulty with what we were doing was that everything that was drawn on the chalkboard was two dimensional. Some things drawn on the chalkboard were two-dimensional drawings of three-dimensional objects. I thought this probably added to the confusion. It definitely made things more confusing for me.

I saw Jennifer, who had been unusually quiet this day, raise her hand. I made a space for her in the conversation, "Jennifer, do you have something you want to say?" "Yeah," she replied, "I don't understand what Ron and the others are talking about. What is a dimension?" Jennifer sounded sincere, as though she really wanted to know. I admired her courage for asking. I asked her to repeat it. "I don't understand what Ron and the others are talking about. They said a dimension. I want to know what a dimension is." Jennifer asked a fundamental question, a type that rarely gets asked or explored in schools.

After Class

By the time I talked with Reineke that afternoon, I wondered what it was that I understood about dimensions. I said, "I don't know about you, but right now I feel so confused about what dimensions are" (Reineke interview, 10/18/89). I had lost the reason we were pursuing a discussion of dimensions. As eager as I had been to pursue dimensions, I was ready to drop them. Why had I followed Ron in the first place? How do you decide which ideas to pursue? I had not figured out that part of this teaching yet. I talked to Reineke about how I thought Lampert might help me.

> One of things that I did with Maggie was to look at her tapes of teaching and I would stop them and ask her why she did this or what she was thinking when she asked that question. I think it would be really interesting for her to watch a tape like this one of today's class . . . maybe she has clues about the mathematics in this discussion. Maybe she could tell me what ideas I could have followed and which ones would have been a good idea to drop.

I wondered what role my own knowledge of dimensions played in this discussion. I asked Reineke:

> I am wondering if the reason that I am floundering with this and I don't know what to do, is it because my own knowledge of dimensions is not helping me, that I am missing that and is that why I don't know where to steer this?

I should have known the limit of my own mathematical knowledge would catch up with me. It always did. Geometry had always seemed like a frill in the years I taught elementary school mathematics. It came at the end of the textbook and at the end of the school year, if there was time. To be doing anything resembling geometry with children in October seemed like giving it some of the increased attention the reforms emphasized.

LABELS

In the next math class, I decided it was time to make the labels. I began class by placing four sheets of brightly colored construction paper in the center of each group of desks as students took cans, scissors, strings, and rulers from their desks. Over the clanging of cans, I heard students choosing the color of construction paper they wanted. I just watched. I saw Sipho equipped with more than the necessary supplies. He noticed me watching. He smiled and held up his bendable ruler. I smiled back and silently wondered if his father would ever see it again. The pitch in the room seemed high. The students were visibly excited. I begged students to please keep the cans quiet for just a few more moments. I wanted to discuss their plans for making labels.

I assumed students would either measure the height and circumference of their cans again or use the measurements they made and recorded the day before. I wanted them to make a record of the measurements on a rectangle they drew in their notebooks and then use the measurements to cut the size of the label needed. The process, however, did not seem so obvious to Wu Lee.

> *Wu Lee:* Do you make them [labels] very small or very big?
> *Ms. Heaton:* What do you think?
> *Wu Lee:* I think make them big because, do we have to cut them out?

Ms. Heaton: What do you think?
Wu Lee: I don't know.

I called on Bob, who looked eager to respond to Wu Lee. Bob explained what could be done with the construction paper, "Well, like you could, like when you take it like, you put it to the very bottom of your can and to the very top of your can and then you take it around and then when it is here you get it and then you cut all of it that's around it and then you fasten it to the can." He was right. Wrapping the paper around the can and cutting the extra off was a way to make a label. But doing it this way did not draw on any of the ideas we had explored over the previous 4 days. It was important to me that they try to use what they had learned about measuring a can to make their labels.

Jennifer spoke up. "I disagree. You can just look on your paper, see what you wrote, measure it with this [the ruler] and cut what is left over and then it will be much easier than having to wrap it [the paper] around and try to cut the thing." I assumed her way seemed easier to her as she imagined the struggle to wrap the paper around the can, hold it in place with one hand, and cut around the can with a pair of scissors in her other hand. I told the students Jennifer and Bob had both come up with viable ways to make a label. I said, "I want you to try to come up with a way of using the measurements of height and circumference to figure out how to make the label for the can." I was learning that I could never assume that connections I saw across days and within activities were obvious to anyone else. Part of my role was to make them explicit. Sometimes this meant identifying students like Jennifer to help me.

After promising to measure, students began making labels. I walked from one cluster of desks to the next and watched and listened as students worked. Something I saw a student do reminded me that I had forgotten part of the directions. I raised my voice above the students' talk and said, "I want to add one more thing. When you make your label—can I borrow someone's paper for a minute?—I want you to try to make it so that when it wraps around the can the edges just meet. I do not want them to overlap." I held up the paper and said, "See the difference between them just meeting and overlapping?" Luke asked, "But why don't you want us to overlap?"

I realized what I was instructing students to do was not the way real labels were attached to cans. They overlapped. But I continued and in an authoritative voice said, "Because I would like you to try to get them to meet." Sipho pushed me. "Well, if they do not overlap, how are we going to fasten them to the can?" He had a point. "You will be able to put a piece of tape across the back," I said in a tone that implied there would be no further discussion. The students went back to work.

Never Mind the Millimeters

I wondered if I should have told them the real reason why I wanted them to make labels that did not overlap. This is from the teacher's guide.

> *T*: Today we're going to make labels for cans you've brought. We'll try to make the labels so that they just fit the cans—so that they don't overlap themselves. What measurements of the cans will we need to make? (McREL, 1986, p. 7)

It did not say why students should make labels that did not overlap. I constructed my own reason. I wanted students to make labels and judge the accuracy of their own measurements. The point of the lesson was to measure the labels in centimeters and when they did not fit, see that measuring in millimeters, a smaller unit, would lead to a more accurate, better fitting label. Here is what was noted a bit later in the teacher's guide.

> After everyone has cut out a label, discuss possible problems with size.
>
> T: Some of you found that your labels did not fit quite right. The label might have been too wide, too short, or too long. You may or may not have tried to make an adjustment. What might have been some reasons for the size differences?
>
> Accept reasonable comments. If no one suggests or hints at size problems caused by measuring to the nearest centimeter, mention it yourself. (McREL, 1986, p. 10)

I was uncertain whether we would get to a discussion of millimeters. I would be satisfied if everyone got labels made and we had assessed their fit. I had already decided that I would move on to something new the next day no matter what happened that day. Five days seemed like plenty of time to have spent on this. I wanted to end with the feel that there was still more to learn.

It took students most of the class period to make labels. After Sipho brought it to our attention a few days earlier that five people got five different measurements of the same can, it looked as if most people did not trust their first measurement. I saw many students measure cans multiple times before measuring and cutting construction paper. With 15 minutes until lunch, I pushed students to finish. I wanted the last 10 minutes to discuss what they had done.

The activity turned out just as the teacher's guide had predicted: Most labels did not fit. Some were off by a few centimeters, while others were off by millimeters. I had to do some fast talking with several students who looked upset that their labels did not quite fit. They thought they had done bad work. I needed to convince them otherwise. I asked them to tell me why they thought their label was the wrong size and how they would make it differently if they were to do it again. Each person had ideas about the source of their errors and had already come up with remedies if they were to try it again. I told them their answers to those questions mattered more to me than whether their label fit.

I decided to repeat this conversation of what mattered to me with the whole group and dismissed the idea of talking about millimeters. There were only 10 minutes remaining and I did not want anyone leaving feeling unsuccessful. From my perspective, the past 5 days of making labels for cans represented the best of math this year. But I saw it that way only when I redefined the meaning of success. Given the richness of the discussions of the past few days, I did not mind if we never discussed millimeters, even though it was the point of the lesson from the perspective of the teacher's guide. In a similar way, I wanted students to feel successful because of what they had learned in spite of the fact that many labels did not fit.

I asked several students to share how they were now thinking about their labels. They talked about the process of making their labels, showed what resulted, and described what they would do differently if they were to make labels again. It was a time to share and listen as students evaluated their own work. In the midst of the talk, the lunch bell rang. Before I could say anything, someone asked if they could take the cans home now that the labels had been made. "No," I said, "Please keep them in your desk. We might use them again." After class, I admitted to the classroom teacher that I had no immediate plans for making use of the cans again. I just did not feel right about letting them go, at least not that day.

After Class

Reineke did not observe on the day we made labels. When I talked to him a day later, I explained how I felt.

Heaton: Yesterday, that was the end of the cans.
Reineke: Yeah?
Heaton: But, not really the end of the cans, I don't think.
Reineke: Why?
Heaton: I don't feel like it has ended.
Reineke: You'll come back to the cans?
Heaton: I think so. I don't know how or what I'll do with them but I don't feel, I don't want to send those cans home.
Reineke: Why?
Heaton: I mean I don't want to send them home now because that somehow signals an end.

It felt more like a beginning. Accompanying the excitement of a new sense for improvisation, came a new set of challenges I needed to better understand concerning children, curriculum, and teaching.

CHAPTER 6

Learning to Share the Dance with Students

I revisit the previous moments of improvisation and reinterpret them from my current perspective. I use the image and language of improvisational dance (Blom & Chaplin, 1988; Novack, 1990) as a tool for my analysis here. This metaphor enriches the image of improvisation in teaching as it focuses on the interdependent relationship among the participants. I try to understand the nature of the collective improvisation students and I are learning to do.

LEARNING THE PURPOSE OF DANCING

My efforts to understand the exchange around rectangles (see Chapter 5) has become an occasion for me to more deeply understand what it means to engage with intellectual ideas in the context of teaching and learning mathematics for understanding. John's struggle with language as he attempted to define a rectangle and his interactions with others around his conjecture is an opportunity to further my understanding of mathematical proof and the demands placed on participants engaged in mathematical argument.

David's offer of a counterexample is a perfectly defensible move, mathematically. Proof or ways of verifying, justifying, and accepting something as reasonable knowledge (Lakatos, 1976) are important aspects of doing mathematics. What David came up with fits John's initial conjecture ("If two ends are the same size, like if two ends are little and two ends are littler than the other two ends.") but reveals some hidden assumptions. After hearing what David had to say, John revised his conjecture by adding the condition that there were four, not five, "ends." Lakatos refers to what John did as "the method of monster-barring" (p. 23). "Using this method," Lakatos writes, "one can eliminate any counterexample to the original conjecture by a sometimes deft and always ad hoc redefinition" (p. 23). David posed an interpretation of John's definition that led to a different figure (what Lakatos would call a "monster") than John intended. As a way of dealing with this "monster," John revised his definition of a rectangle, thereby eliminating the "monster." David, however, was not through. He revealed yet another of John's hidden assumptions. David took an eraser, removed the fifth side, and said, "There, that has four ends."

Interpreting the Dance

At the time, I was uncertain what to make of John's exchange with David. One interpretation of what David did is that he played the "refutationist" (Lakatos, 1976), someone who calls attention to possible "unintended interpretations" (p. 84). He interpreted John's conjecture in ways that stretched the meaning of the conjecture to include shapes beyond what John intended. The outcome of this was that David's method of surfacing unintended meanings moved John to be more explicit about what he did intend. Mathematically, this was a good thing to have happen. However, a second interpretation of what David did was that he looked for ways to point out John's errors for the purpose of embarrassing John. In one case, the aim was to further the mathematical thinking of the group. In the other case, the aim was to humiliate John. Given what I know about the boys' relationship as well as their mathematical ability, both were reasonable possibilities. In such situations, teachers need to sense the feel of the interaction, or read the "tenor of the discourse" (Atweh, Bleicher, & Cooper, 1998) and, based on a complex set of variables, decide what to do next. In this case, my decision and subsequent action were based on a host of reasons related to my knowledge of these individual students, my sense of the class dynamic that was developing around their interactions, and my concerns for the mathematical progress of the group as a whole as well as the well-being of individuals at any given moment. Acquiring a clearer sense of the role of disagreement in doing mathematics, and the potential benefits and risks for the participants, would help me to make the moment-to-moment, student-by-student decisions demanded in this and other situations.

Appreciating Mathematical Arguments

Argument is a way for mathematical ideas to develop. But I am learning the reasons are broader than that. The similarities in the way I want students to learn to do mathematics connect to the ways in which I want them to engage with intellectual ideas in any other subject. Fawcett (1938), writing about the nature of proof, addresses some broader purposes.

> What these teachers really want is not only that these young people understand the nature of proof but that their way of life should show that they understand it. Of what value is it for a pupil to understand thoroughly what a proof means if it does not clarify his thinking and make him more "critical of new ideas presented"? The real value of this sort of training to any pupil is determined by its effect on his behavior, and for purposes of this study we shall assume that if he clearly understands these aspects of the nature of proof his behavior will be marked by the following characteristics:
>
> 1. He will select the significant words and phrases in any statement that is important to him and ask that they be carefully defined.
> 2. He will require evidence in support of any conclusion he is pressed to accept.
> 3. He will analyze that evidence and distinguish fact from assumption.
> 4. He will recognize stated and unstated assumptions essential to the conclusion.
> 5. He will evaluate these assumptions, accepting some and rejecting others.
> 6. He will evaluate the argument, accepting or rejecting the conclusion.
> 7. He will constantly re-examine the assumptions which are behind his beliefs and which guide his actions. (pp. 11–12)

In light of these broader purposes, one can begin to see how this series of lessons was about so much more than making labels for cans, and the time spent becomes justifiable. My own learning is as multifaceted as the children's. On one level, I am learning how to work with students to define rectangles. On another level, I am learning how to work with students to have mathematical arguments. On yet another level, I am learning how to work with students for the purpose of engaging in intellectual ideas. What is learned here is not preparation for something else; it is learning a way of being, of engaging with other people and ideas, of living as a member in a democracy (Dewey, 1916/1966). Similarly, improvisational dance is not done just for the purpose of entertaining an audience. Pleasure and satisfaction occur for dancers in the doing of the dance. It is important as well to recognize more than a utilitarian view for engaging in mathematical arguments and discussions. This is a view of the purpose of teaching mathematics for understanding that goes beyond an application of problem solving to the real world. Thinking and arguing about ideas have value in and of themselves.

LEARNING TO USE TEXTBOOKS AND STUDENTS AS RESOURCES

In my past teaching, I always gave directions and students were supposed to follow them. The point was to get through directions as quickly as possible and move on to the task. My attitudes about what is worth spending time on are changing. In my continual search for interesting mathematical ideas to discuss, I have been learning to have a new appreciation of the directions for a task as a site for mathematical exploration. Directions for a task usually are based on an implicit set of assumptions about a proper way to perform a task as well the right outcome or product. Once directions are themselves questions, the process becomes open to interpretation and part of the task.

Questioning the Authority

Questioning instructions in the teacher's guide became a way for me to begin to take some control of the content. I am learning that students can do the same, if given the chance. The exchange with Sipho over making the labels so they do not overlap is an example in which Sipho questioned my directions. But because I am the teacher, I have more authority. When exercised, that authority can stifle students' attempts to make meaning for themselves. The ways in which I am trying to renegotiate my position with the textbook and its authority is similar to what students are trying to learn to do with me. In a sense, their work ought not be any more about blindly following directions than mine is. While I negotiate a new relationship with a teacher's guide, students are learning to negotiate a new relationship with me.

For example, we spent much of the class period from which the episode "Strings" is drawn dealing with directions for making labels. The question of how to measure a can with a string was the focus. Here is what the directions in the CSMP teacher's guide said.

> Measure to the nearest centimeter the circumference for your can and its height. Use a metric tape measure, or cut pieces of string in the appropriate lengths and then measure the string. (McREL, 1986, p. 8)

There is a risk in opening up directions like this to interpretation. It means moving away from the teacher's guide and hoping that something useful will come from the venture. I could feel that as my dependence on the teacher's guide was decreasing, my dependence on students was increasing. For example, I had a hunch that the directions and the string could lead to something interesting, but I could not be certain how the lesson would turn out until I tried it. A lot was riding on how these students would make sense of measuring the can.

I am learning to see students as integral players in all that I attempt to do as a teacher. Not only do I need something interesting for students to talk about, but I am dependent on their involvement. Cohen (1988) writes about how such adventurous teaching makes distinctive demands on teachers. It requires that teachers "depend on students to produce an unusually large share of instruction" (p. 58). It also means learning to trust that students each have something to offer and that together we will construct mathematical meaning out of a task. I want students to appreciate the process at least as much as the product. As the teacher, I have the responsibility to look for tasks that hold the potential for engaging students in meaningful mathematics.

I also am learning that I have to recognize students' potential: that not only do students have more to offer than I ever knew, but that what they have to offer is always changing. By the middle of October, when these lessons occurred, I knew the students fairly well. I had a sense of who they were as individuals, the nature of their personalities, and the shape of their relationships with one another. I also had a sense for what they understood about mathematics. There were certain things that I came to expect of each of them. Fixed expectations did something to ease my uncertainty, but at times my expectations blinded me to students' growing potential. I needed to free my expectations to be as dynamic and evolving as students' growth and development, because I used what I knew about individual students as one means of guiding my actions during discussions. Decisions about whom to call on were based on reasons that included the feel of the moment, what the other students were doing, what mathematical ideas I wanted to teach, what ideas I had for teaching them, how much time had passed and remained in the math class, where we had been, where we were at the moment, and where we were headed.

Embracing Uncertainty

The complex dynamics and many influencing factors of the teacher–student relationship are not something explicitly addressed in CSMP. In places where typical student answers are listed in response to a teacher question, there is no indication that the relationship between the teacher and student and among students plays a role in the learning of mathematics. Here is how the interaction among participants is represented in the CSMP teacher's guide.

T: Question
S: Response
S: Response
S: Response

This means a teacher question often is followed by three possible student responses. The responses come from real classroom experiences or were considered mathematically interesting by the curriculum designers. While I am certain CSMP intended for these relationships to be more complex than they appear here, I am not certain the curriculum designers see them playing as central a role in the learning of mathematics as I propose. I was not dealing with generic fourth graders. These were real students with real growing and changing personalities and abilities that played a central role in my teaching.

The fact that I am dealing with growing, changing human beings and I am one myself contributes to the inherent uncertainty in my job as a teacher (Cohen, 1988). Sometimes students respond as I predict; other times they do not. Sometimes the unpredictability leads to exciting new places, other times to dead ends. Sometimes it takes me longer to see where we are headed than others. Are there ways a teacher's guide can help me deal with the uncertainty? Its certainty was not helping me deal with the uncertainty of this kind of teaching. I found myself, oddly enough, looking to students. I was learning to see students not only as the source of the difficulties I confronted in this teaching but as resources for dealing with them.

My first exchange with Sipho over the discrepancies in classmates' measurements of the same can is a good example of my coming to see a student as a resource. It was an unpredictable exchange that led in a totally unexpected, surprisingly productive direction that almost did not happen because of my fixed expectations of Sipho and my momentary drive to make progress on the task of making the labels. I happened to make the space for Sipho's idea and was amazed by his insightfulness. I worry about how many times I did not bother. And I worry about the reasons why this might have happened. Did it have to do with students' color or gender or what I perceived as their mathematical abilities? I am not sure that I know the answers as a teacher, nor do I have the data to study these questions here as a scholar. What I am learning is that they are important questions to ask as I learn to consider the potential of all students as resources.

Sipho's curiosity and willingness to raise the question moved the whole group forward by bridging our past experiences of measuring and the inaccuracy of the process with the measuring all students were about to do. For a moment, I observed Sipho step into the role of teacher. For a moment, he was a teacher in ways similar to the moment I experienced as a teacher with Arif in Chapter 3. He heard what students said, connected what he heard to the mathematical idea of measurement, and responded with a thought-provoking question. I was learning students could be teachers. They, too, could be improvisers. They only needed to be given the opportunity. To give students opportunities to be teachers means that I, as the teacher, need to be prepared to be responsive, spontaneous, and willing to take risks, and put myself in the role of a learner. Just when I thought I was able to predict a student's response, I was taken by surprise. But it is the surprises, I am learning, that can be opportunities for teaching and learning. And those surprises often come from students I least expect them from when I structure my work to allow for that to happen. I am learning to embrace uncertainty so that students and I can move along in this teaching together, with the direction constructed jointly as we go.

LEARNING TO SHARE THE LEAD

Dealing with the surprises that I am learning are an important part of this teaching and learning evokes a range of emotion. At times the surprises feel threatening, like when a student sees something I overlooked. This was the case with Sipho and what he made of his observations of students' measurements. A first impulse could have been to stifle him and hide the fact that I was learning from him. He saw something I did not. I was coming to see that celebrating insights, even when they were not my own, could benefit the whole group. If I could say that a student had helped me to see something that otherwise would have gone unnoticed for me, I would be offering a powerful model for the kind of learning from one another that I wanted students to be doing.

The surprises of teaching may not always be timed the way I might want them to be, as was the case with Sipho's bendable ruler. From Sipho's perspective it was perfectly timed. It came the day after he noticed the inaccuracy of the measurements with string and understood the difficulties presented by an ordinary ruler. A bendable ruler is ingenious. But I know few teachers who appreciate any surprise, ingenious or not, when revealed moments before they are about to teach, a time when their minds are filled with their own plans for what they are about to do. Altering my plans and letting Sipho open the class with a demonstration of his bendable ruler was a signal to the group that I was willing to share the lead with him, of all people, someone with whom I had always felt like I was competing for attention. Through this exchange, I came to see Sipho in a new light. I had always perceived him as a follower. He did anything to be accepted and wanted desperately to be heard. Giving up the lead to him seemed like a way to begin to meet his needs and allow him to construct a different role for himself. Is it just a coincidence that Sipho and I had a relationship filled with friction and he also had troubles with his peers? How much influence can I, as the teacher, have over how students are perceived by their peers? What did my show of respect for Sipho and my move to give him the lead do for our relationship and his relationship with his peers? Learning to share the leadership with students was not easy to do. It required that I feel confident enough in what I was doing to give up control. I was learning that giving up control was actually a sign of being in control, something both teachers and students need to learn.

LEARNING WHICH LEADS AND LEADERS TO FOLLOW

I was excited when I first heard Ron's elaborate explanation of dimensions (see Chapter 5) and thought his ideas might hold the potential to take us to interesting mathematical places. But when I started the next class period with Ron reviewing his definition, he seemed much less clear about his understanding of dimensions than I had first assessed. What I thought was a deep understanding of dimensions was actually quite fragile and formalistic. I started to worry that rather than providing an opportunity for Ron to shine, I had unwittingly put him in an embarrassing position. At the time, I felt as if we were moving in circles with the mathematics and backing Ron into a corner.

As I look back on this now, I can see more clearly a layer of social issues that sits on top of the talk of dimensions. In looking back over the conversation I had with Reineke around this lesson, I was reminded of the interplay between mathematical content and social interaction.

Heaton: Did you notice Ron's posture? I guess that's maybe what I would want to look at on the tape—how it changes throughout the class. At another point he is sort of sitting back in his chair with his arm on the counter, and my thought when I saw him like that was he feels, it was a posture like he was saying, "I will just let these people talk but I know that what I am saying is right."

Reineke: O.K., what does that say about the construction of knowledge?

Heaton: That maybe it had ended at that point for him . . . I am just not sure how much other people's ideas were affecting his ideas.

Reineke: Is that important?

Heaton: I think that is important. Because it seems like there could be a two-way thing also to the degree that his, other people's ideas are affecting his and how are his ideas influencing someone else—it seemed like that sort of stopped or something. I just found the whole thing really interesting both body movements and ideas. The way they were sharing their ideas and the implications underlying these things.

Reineke: What does Ron's pompousness, sitting back in his chair putting his elbow up and things like that and kind of gazing over the masses . . . what does that do or how does that affect conjecture and refutation as part of mathematical dialogue?

Heaton: I think then that people might be addressing that feeling that he is giving off rather than really thinking about his ideas.

Reineke: Does it say anything about Ron's authority of knowledge?

Heaton: Ron thinks he has the authority . . . rather than, "We are going to figure this out together."

I was not sure what to do during the lesson. I regretted my move. I did not know enough about dimensions at the time myself to take back the lead I had given Ron. I could not figure out how to make a graceful link back to the cans nor could I figure out how to help Ron save face.

Jennifer saved us. She said what I think many were thinking at the time. She said she did not understand what was being talked about. She and I were both lost in a discussion of multiple dimensions when neither she nor I was sure of the definition of a dimension. She had the courage to say she did not understand something and, in the process, she cut to the core of the difficulty of the discussion and put a halt to our spinning. She asked a fundamental question that sits at the middle of confusion as well as understanding. Her question allowed me to put the question of dimensions gracefully on hold and turn attention away from Ron. Maybe we would return to the topic as a group. Maybe students would meet ideas about dimensions on their own. And, if they did, maybe they would recall this discussion and be able to make new sense of it. In any case, we did not have to spend any more time with the idea then and could return to making labels for cans.

I was learning that some improvised moments, like this one, lead nowhere in particular, or at least at the time they appear this way. Some may be recalled later and lead somewhere in the future. Others will never be touched again. I was still not very good at recognizing which ones were which. And I also was learning that this was not just a dance of ideas. These ideas belonged to children, whose feelings and attitudes needed to be constantly read in the course of our dance.

LEARNING TO ASSESS MY OWN PROGRESS

CSMP intended this one-day lesson on making labels for cans to be one in which students would make labels that did not fit and see that measuring in millimeters would lead to a more accurate measurement than measuring in centimeters. This point actually was made only in the midst of our fifth day of working with these cans, in a private conversation with one student. I view these 5 days as a success and I base my assessment on what I saw accomplished with students. I have a sense where we started and where we ended up. We made our own meaning out of the activity. The fact that our meaning did not match CSMP's does not take away from its success. This was a new way for me to be thinking about success and progress. Improvisational teaching and the process of mathematical thinking cannot be assessed with answer books alone.

Self-assessment was something students were learning to deal with as well. Many students thought they had done poorly because their labels did not fit. I needed to convince these students that whether or not their labels fit was not the point. A lot had been learned to get to this point, and they all had ideas of what they would do differently, if they were to make these labels over again. I found myself trying to convince students of ways of assessing their own learning that I was only beginning to understand in terms of my own teaching.

Are there expectations of what students are to learn in an area like geometry that are different from other areas they are to learn about, like multiplication and division, for example? Something I found in CSMP leads me to think that CSMP sees a difference. A benefit of the Geometry and Measurement strand, from CSMP's perspective (McREL, 1986), is that it provides alternative opportunities for mathematical reasoning. Geometric reasoning in the context of spatial and measurement activities provides an alternative area for the success of students for whom numerical reasoning is a challenge.

> The focus of this strand is on experience . . . no goals for mastery can be listed here. The effects of such an informal approach must be judged by

> the long term effects on the students' knowledge, confidence, intuition, and interest in the world of geometry and measurement. (McREL, 1986, p. vi)

This less serious focus on the content may be what allowed me to get a feel for the complex teacher–student and student–student interactions. A mix of content and process goals is central to this kind of teaching.

LEARNING TO DANCE

What I am learning here is that my interactions with students and the mathematics are about being in control and taking or giving up control at a moment's notice. The dance metaphor is helpful in explaining what I mean. In the language of improvisational dance, being in control means "being centered" and this means being "responsive and ready" (Blom & Chaplin, 1988, p. 31), prepared to "give or take weight, to support, to resist, or to yield, as called for by the interaction" (Novack, 1990, p. 128). I am learning about a way of being with students and subject matter that is ever-changing and uncertain. I cannot decide until I am in the situation what my next move will be. This is very different from the way I used to teach mathematics. Traditional dance is such that you learn the moves or steps and as the music plays you do the right steps, repeating them over and over, in a rote fashion. Jackson (1986) gives the example of dance lessons, such as these, as the closest example he can think of to "pure mimetic teaching." This is much closer to the way I learned mathematics and taught it when I followed the textbook.

Improvisational dance offers a completely different image. Improvisational dancers prepare themselves to be in the situation with other dancers and decide in the moment, based on their feel for their interactions with other dancers, what to do next.

> In contact improvisation, each person is conceived of as an individual yet cannot do the dance unless it is shared with another. Contact improvisation defines the self as the responsive body and also as the responsive body listening to another responsive body, the two together spontaneously creating a third force that directs the dance. The boundaries of the individual are crossed by "seeing through the body" and "listening through the skin," allowing the dance to unfold. (Novack, 1990, p. 189)

As Novack's (1990) book title, *Sharing the Dance*, implies, the students and teacher are not just learning to dance as individuals. Collectively, they are learning to share the dance. Understanding the nature of this partnership is not easy, though. For while it is true they are learning to share the dance, the teacher still has responsibilities that differ from those of students. The image of the role of the leader of a group of improvisational dancers seems useful in understanding certain aspects of the teacher's role and responsibilities.

> Your job is to insure that the conditions conducive to such a response are present. It is for you to generate an atmosphere where explorations, experiments, and risks can take place safely. You must see that each person is accepted, respected and dealt with equally; that no one is judged or compared; and that each mover is helped to shape his experience so as to make it meaningful for him. (Blom & Chaplin, 1988, p. 54)

Next, I needed to figure out how to attend to the intricacies of the process and pay serious attention to content.

CHAPTER 7

What Should I Do Next?

Every teacher is faced with the question, "What do I do next?" Here I deal with the question during four lessons in April and a day of math class at the end of the year. In contemplating the question of what to do next, I find myself learning to integrate what I have learned, as described in the previous chapters: how to listen and respond to students in the situation, to rely less on the CSMP teacher's guide regarding how and what to teach, and to give up some control of the content and conversation to students. I do this as I struggle to understand the mathematical territory of fractions.

Nearly 6 months have elapsed between the series of lessons studied in this chapter and those lessons described and analyzed in Chapters 5 and 6. In the interim, I taught an introductory course in teacher education at the university. I no longer followed CSMP closely or exclusively. I had begun to take much more responsibility for answering the question of what to do next. I was frustrated with the spiral organization of the CSMP curriculum, which switches from one content strand to another from one day to the next. During my break, I had been considering ways to reorganize the curriculum so that I could stay with a single topic over several days. I wrote in my journal, "I am very frustrated with CSMP at this point. This jumping around from topic to topic doesn't fit with what I am trying to do. I am thinking about how to reorganize" (Heaton journal, 04/10/90).

THE RAIN PROBLEM

As I planned this math lesson in mid-April, I wanted to continue with the topic of fractions we had begun several days earlier. I searched for a problem that would require adding fractions with like denominators and provide a challenge for those who could already add fractions. I found one in the Addison-Wesley textbook (Eicholz, O'Daffer, Feelnor, Charles, Young, & Barnett, 1987) that seemed appropriate and manageable.

> On Saturday it rained $^{3}/_{8}$ of an inch. On Sunday it rained $^{7}/_{8}$ of an inch. How much did it rain in the two days? (p. 251)

My reason for choosing a particular problem had become part of what I wrote in the journal where I now kept my reflections on lessons as well as my plans for future lessons.

> I chose the problem because I want to stick with fractions. In the lessons I've been doing on finding fractions of a whole number, addition and subtraction of fractions has come up. So, I think they need a bit more of a challenge. This problem allows them to add fractions but also gives those who are ready the opportunity to think about something more—the numerator larger than the denominator, leading us into mixed numbers. It also seems like the opportunity to talk about where fractions fall on the number line. (Heaton journal, 04/11/90)

How Would I Solve the Problem?

I found myself rethinking my own understanding of the mathematics I was asking students to learn. How would I make sense of the meaning of adding fractions? Drawing a picture might help. While I would leave children to their own devices, I imagined some might draw a rain gauge. I assumed they would divide it into eighths, start at $^{3}/_{8}$, add $^{7}/_{8}$ more, and find $^{10}/_{8}$ as the solution. I thought the challenge would be to see $^{10}/_{8}$ as greater than an inch or equivalent to one whole inch of rain plus $^{2}/_{8}$ of an inch.

Students sat at desks arranged in groups of four and talked quietly as they worked. On that particular day, their talk sounded as if it was about the math problem. This was not always the case. Some days I heard the buzz of their voices and was fooled into thinking they were working together until I listened more closely and heard anything but mathematics being discussed. In the past it had been much easier to make judgments about students' engagement. They were either talking and off task or working and silent. Silence, however, was no longer a goal. Talking in meaningful ways about mathematical ideas had taken its place.

There were reasons for listening closely to students that went beyond judging on- and off-task behavior. I used what I heard to help me decide what to do next. I borrowed a structure that I had observed in Lampert's class that supported the listening and decision making in action that I was learning to do. Lampert started each class with a single math problem. Students could choose to work alone or with the people with whom they were sitting. This provided more than just an alternative way to organize a math class. Roaming the room and eavesdropping while students worked in small groups was a way to get some sense of students' mathematical understandings and figure out what to do next.

Multiple Representations

I was amazed by the variety of pictures they had drawn. The pictures were mainly a collection of shaded rectangles and circles that looked very different from the rain gauge I had imagined. What did they understand about the process of measuring rainfall? It was a context that made sense to the writers of the word problem and it made sense to me, but what sense did it make to these fourth graders? Imagining a picture I might draw forced me to consider my own solution to the problem, but did not prepare me for these other points of view.

To build on the variety of students' work I observed, I asked five students to draw their pictures on the chalkboard. We had time to discuss three of these in the remaining 20 minutes of class (see Figure 7.1).

Naruj's Perspective. A stranger might wonder what Naruj's picture had to do with figuring out the rain problem, but I recognized its representational logic, although I was puzzled by Naruj's reasoning. It was similar to students' drawings done over the past several days to figure out fractions of whole numbers. Naruj's answer was $^{10}/_{8}$ of 16, which was the same as 20. Although I am uncertain where he got the 16 from, it is logical to divide 16 into eight equal groups of two each. One eighth of 16 is 2; Naruj's picture shows 8 groups of 2, or 16; $^{10}/_{8}$ of 16 is found by adding two eighths of 16 (or 4) to 16, which equals 20. Naruj's statement that $^{10}/_{8}$ of 16 equals 20 was correct but it was unclear to me how he saw this as related to the rain problem.

Bob's Perspective. Although Bob's picture was not included on the chalkboard, I include his contribution to the discussion here to illustrate what was revealed as the students tried to solve the rainfall problem. Bob thought the solution was $^{10}/_{16}$ and explained why.

> Well, I knew it says three eighths of an inch and seven eighths of an inch and I knew it could not be higher than two inches be-

FIGURE 7.1: Students' Representations

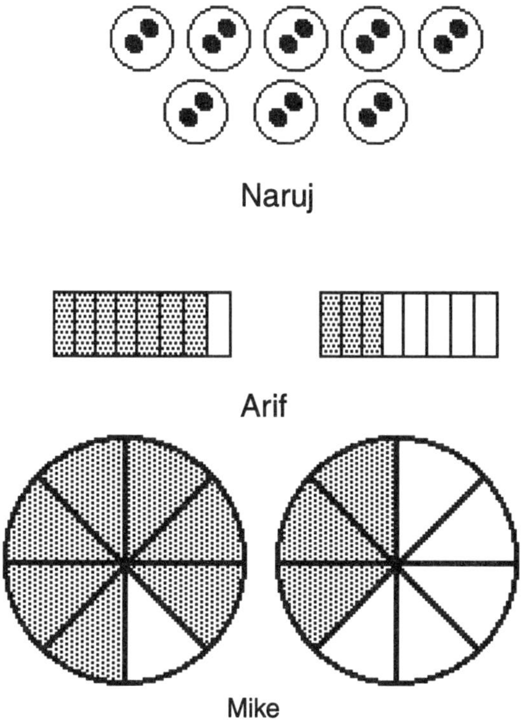

cause it says three eighths of *an inch*. I mean there are 16 millimeters in an inch and I mean there are only three millimeters that we are using in one eighth so I knew it could not be higher than one inch. Actually, I thought it couldn't be higher than an inch because we are only using three out of 16 and seven out of 16 and that is only 10.

As I heard Bob's mix of inches, millimeters, and fractions of inches and saw a ruler in his hand, I felt frustrated. I had not considered using a ruler. If I had, I would have warned students to stay clear of metric measurements. Students frequently confused metric and standard units. Sixteen might have seemed reasonable to him because it matched the denominator if the 8s were added together. He also might have counted the shortest lines between the 0 and 1 on the inch side of his ruler, hit upon 16 sixteenths, and called them millimeters.

Arif's Perspective. Arif agreed the answer was $\frac{10}{16}$. He explained how looking at his picture one way represented $1\frac{2}{8}$, while looking at it another way represented $\frac{10}{16}$. "Well, they add up to be the same. Like I had seven eighths right here. Well, I had to get three more eighths so I colored this space in and that is one whole and then I colored two here and that is one whole and two eighths." I asked, "What about 10 sixteenths?" Arif said, "Well, I did the same thing except I did not put this line here (see Figure 7.2). I put it over here and just added them like I said, like it is 16 spaces all over here and 10 are colored in." I was amazed Arif was able to view his picture in terms of eighths as well as sixteenths. If I viewed the two rectangles together as the whole, as he did in the his second explanation, I could see $\frac{10}{16}$. If I saw each rectangle as one whole, I could see $1\frac{2}{8}$ of two rectangles. What should I do with Arif's sound explanation of a wrong solution? Could I let students think the solution was $\frac{10}{16}$?

Mike's perspective. Mike agreed with Arif and disagreed with Naruj. I was content until I realized he thought Naruj's answer was $\frac{10}{8}$. He said:

> Naruj, you can't get 10 eighths because if you get 10 eighths you are going to have one whole and two eighths just like me and Arif got. Because if you have seven eighths all you need is one more eighth, one eighth to fill that in and that would be one whole. You can't go over eight eighths.

FIGURE 7.2: Arif's Representation

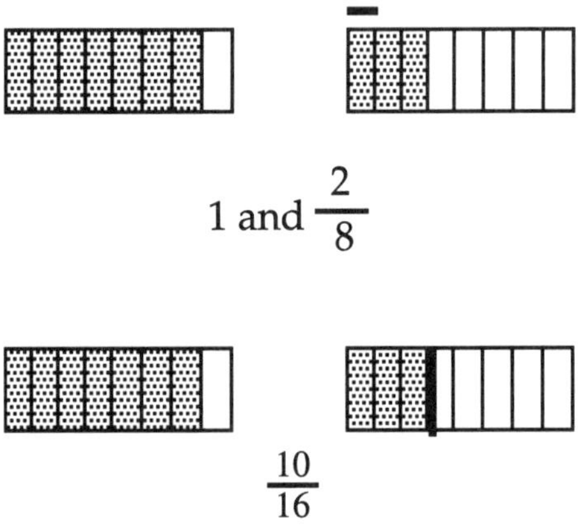

It was good he thought $\frac{10}{8}$ was equivalent to $1\frac{2}{8}$, but where had he gotten the idea the answer could not "go over eight eighths"? I deliberately chose this problem because the answer was more than $\frac{8}{8}$ or one whole. I was curious to hear more from Mike so I asked him to elaborate. He said, "I think it is one and two eighths because like eight eighths is your whole." He pointed to his picture (see Figure 7.1).

He continued, "I am talking about my picture. It is about pies and eight eighths is your whole." He did not seem to notice he had slipped from the language of inches of rain to pieces of pie. "Well you have eight pieces in each pie. Seven pieces are colored in for one of the pies. So you take one of them pieces and you eat that other piece but you don't. You add that in there." I tried to follow what he was saying by moving my fingers from circle to circle and piece of pie to piece of pie. I asked, "Put this one in here?" as I pretended to take one piece from the circle with $\frac{3}{8}$ shaded in and move it to the circle with $\frac{7}{8}$ shaded in. He nodded and said, "And that's your whole. That's eighth eighths of the whole pie. Then you have two eighths left over here of that pie, so it is one and two eighths." What did he mean? How could he say the answer was $1\frac{2}{8}$ but use the argument it was not $\frac{10}{8}$ because it could not go over one? What did he think was the relationship between $\frac{10}{8}$ and $1\frac{2}{8}$? Why was he unable to see it was possible to have a fraction greater than one? What did $\frac{10}{8}$ mean to him? The class ended when the classroom teacher motioned to me that it was already past the time to go to lunch. None of us had heard the bell.

What Next?

A problem with an answer greater than one whole was intended to present a challenge. Instead, it seemed to be viewed as an impossibility. I began to question what anyone knew who I assumed could add fractions. I considered my options for what to do next. I could continue with the rain problem or move to an entirely new topic and leave the addition of fractions behind. While this was tempting, I wanted to try to stick with one topic over consecutive days. I could stay with the topic of adding fractions but find a new problem to work on.

I had felt this way before—not knowing what to do. But it seemed that this time I had gotten myself to this spot differently. Earlier in the year when I tried to follow the script of the teacher's guide closely and students' ideas did not match the teacher's guide, I was at a loss for what to do next. This was different. Here was an example of opening up content and conversation wider around a problem than I had done before. And I was doing it on my own, independent of any teacher's guide. Had I opened things up too far? I was overwhelmed by the deep differences in students' work on the problem. I struggled to understand what was important to learn and why.

I had assumed $\frac{10}{8}$ was an obvious answer to the addition of $\frac{3}{8}$ and $\frac{7}{8}$. I was wrong. If one knows the rule of adding numerators of fractions with like denominators, the answer is obvious. But, what if one were like many of these students and had not learned the rule yet? What were ways to reason about the addition of fractions? I assumed the challenge was to see how $\frac{10}{8}$ could be equivalent to $1\frac{2}{8}$. Instead, some students reasoned the answer was $1\frac{2}{8}$ but saw it as equivalent to $\frac{10}{16}$. Conceptualizing $\frac{10}{8}$ seemed troublesome. I decided to continue with adding fractions but move as far away from rulers and linear measurement as possible.

THE MUFFIN PROBLEM

I found another problem in Addison-Wesley. It situated the addition of fractions in cups of flour rather than inches of rain, a context I hoped would be less messy. I wrote in my journal (04/15/90), "I hope that the unit 'cup of flour' will not complicate the problem like 'inch' did last time, bringing in millimeters and rulers. This got messy." Here is the problem I modified to use the next day.

> One batch of muffins needed $\frac{3}{4}$ cup of flour. The second batch needed $\frac{2}{4}$ cup of flour.
> 1. How much flour was used in both batches?
> 2. How much more flour was used in the first batch than the second batch?
>
> For each problem:
> How do you know?
> Draw a picture.

I watched and listened as students worked. I noticed that students within the same small group appeared to be thinking quite differently. Maybe they could push each other's thinking. I had watched Lampert's students influence each other's thinking daily. Usually to help structure talk within the groups, I suggested each group try to agree on a solution. I stressed "agree" and hoped the task of reaching consensus within a small group would help to limit the range of possible conjectures introduced once the whole-group discussion began. I appreciated the variability of students' ideas but did not always know what to do with them. The small groups never reached consensus. I had not considered the possibility that students with "wrong" answers might have arguments as persuasive as those with "right" answers.

Multiple Conjectures

To narrow the range of ideas, I wanted to begin this whole-group discussion with a simple, clear drawing representative of the "right" answer. David's work caught my eye. He copied on the chalkboard what appeared in his notebook (see Figure 7.3). Afraid we might end up in a mess similar to the one created by the rain problem, I decided to go through features of David's picture with students. I verified that squares represented cups of flour, even though they did not resemble cups of flour. We also discussed why it made sense, given the context of the word problem, to add the cups. When I thought we were clear on squares and reasons for adding, I asked if anyone could explain that four fourths was the same as one. If students could understand that one was equivalent to four fourths, then they might be able to see five fourths as one fourth more than one. Ana had the "right" answer when I talked to her during the small-group time. I called on her, hoping she could explain her understanding of the relationship between four fourths and one. She said, "Because if you have four out of four you have a whole." Bob shot his hand up in the air. I knew the moment I called on Bob, the possibilities of where this might lead would no longer remain in my control.

FIGURE 7.3: David's Work

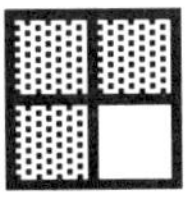 $= \frac{3}{4}$ cup of flour

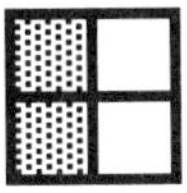 $= \frac{2}{4}$ cup of flour

$\frac{3}{4} + \frac{1}{4} = 1$ cup of flour and $\frac{1}{4}$ cup of flour left over

so you can say $1\frac{1}{4}$

Reluctantly, I nodded in Bob's direction and he said, "I am challenging Ana when she says four fourths equals a cup." I wanted to disagree with him. I knew, however, telling him he was wrong would not necessarily change how he thought. And besides, this teaching was not about right and wrong answers. It was about understanding why answers were right or wrong. I let Bob talk and hoped classmates were listening. He continued, "I am thinking, well it can be a lot of different numbers because of, if you have a circle and you cut it into eight pieces, four fourths isn't the whole of that."

My patience was fading. I drew a circle divided into eighths on the board and asked, "What would four fourths of this circle be?" Bob, in all sincerity, responded, "That would be half of the whole." Outwardly calm and inwardly frustrated, I asked, "Then, what is the whole?" He responded, "One whole is eight eighths." I wanted to push him on the relationship between fourths and eighths, and asked, "What would half of this circle be?" Bob said, "Four eighths." Did that mean he thought four fourths and four eighths were the same thing? I saw Asim's hand. Asim did not speak often, but when he did, he always made thoughtful contributions. He said, "I agree because four eighths means like four things, like four pieces of cake or pie colored in out of eight." I wanted Asim to speak to the idea of four fourths not being half of the whole circle. Rather than follow up directly on Asim's ideas, I called on Mike, whose hand was in the air. He said, "I have something for Bob. Bob, were you thinking about the rain [problem]?" It appeared he was trying to understand Bob's reason for talking about eighths.

Bob responded, "I think four fourths would be the whole when you have fourths but if you were using eighths the whole would be eight eighths." Hearing this, I wanted to think, at least for the moment, this question of whether the whole circle was four fourths or four eighths was settled. We could get back to the question of ¾ plus ²⁄₄. What sort of differences existed in students' answers to this question now? I asked, "Did anyone come up with something different than David who got one and one fourth?" Arif's arm was stretched in the air. "I think this is the same thing. I came up with five eighths," he announced. When I asked him to explain, he drew two circles and divided each into four sections (see Figure 7.4). He continued his explanation, "See, together there's eight pieces in both. Eight pieces of pie in both and I colored in three from here and two from here so I just add the three plus two is five and if you like, you can use this from here and that would be four fourths and one fourth." He motioned with his hand as though he was taking one of the two fourths that had been shaded in the circle and moving it over to fill in the circle with ¾ already

FIGURE 7.4: Arif's Drawing

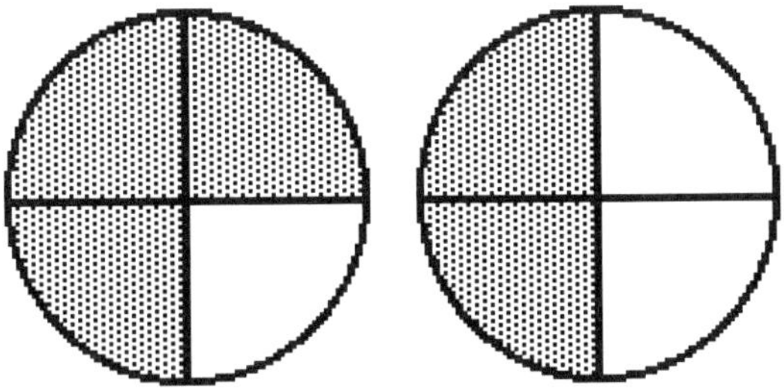

shaded. Did Arif really believe the answer was $\frac{5}{8}$ or $1\frac{1}{4}$? This was similar to what he did the day before when he decided the solution to the rain problem was $\frac{10}{16}$ *or* $1\frac{2}{8}$.

His picture was convincing. Looking at these circles as two wholes, I saw $\frac{5}{4}$. But looking at the two circles as one whole, I could see eight pieces with five shaded in. With that latest conjecture, there were now students who thought the answer was $\frac{5}{4}$, or $1\frac{1}{4}$, and students who thought it was $\frac{5}{8}$. There were also some students who thought $\frac{5}{4}$ was the same as $1\frac{1}{4}$ and others who thought $\frac{5}{8}$ was the same as $1\frac{1}{4}$. What should I do next? Should I just tell them the "right" answer? How would I explain the "right" answer using Arif's picture? Why was the answer was $\frac{5}{4}$ and not $\frac{5}{8}$? *I* wasn't sure.

Bob had more to say.

> I challenge Arif because I agree with the five for the numerator but I challenge what he put for the denominator because we're talking in fourths right now, so when you're talking in fourths we're not using eighths. So I think it is five fourths and also my hypothesis is I think, I can't remember what the name is but those numbers that connect two of them. I think maybe five fourths and one and one fourth might be the same.

He was referring to a conversation we had the week before about equivalent fractions. I said "equivalent fractions," he nodded and continued, "We are talking with fourths, not eighths. I mean then we'd have to switch the three fourths to three eighths, and two fourths to two eighths, so I think it would have to be five fourths." Did he really think $\frac{3}{8}$ was equivalent to $\frac{3}{4}$ and $\frac{2}{4}$ equivalent to $\frac{2}{8}$?

I returned to Arif, who said, "Well, Bob, o.k., we're talking about if, like the first batch, in the first batch there's three fourths, so we're including fourths and then the second batch that's like totally different, it's like two fourths." Bob responded, "Yes, but we're still talking fourths." To which Arif replied, "I know we're still talking about fourths except we're just adding them." Bob continued, "Yes, but when you add fourths, I mean you're getting eighths so then you're going to have to have three eighths and two eighths. So then that would get five eighths but we're talking about fourths, not eighths." Arif said, "Yes, but you're just adding the fourths. Like over there, what do you think the answer is to this?" He pointed to his picture (see Figure 7.4). "I think it would either be one and one fourth or five eighths." I interrupted and said in a questioning tone, "or five eighths," hoping that he meant $5/4$. He said, "Five fourths." I addressed the whole group. "What do other people think here? We've got two ideas—Arif's idea that this is five eighths and Bob's idea that this is five fourths." I intended to open up the conversation to others but noticed Arif. His waving hand told me he had more to say and I gave him another chance to speak. Arif addressed Bob directly, again. "Well, Bob, first of all it can't be five fourths because there's four pieces and you have to color in five of them. How can you do that? You've got four pieces and you're coloring five of them?" On the one hand, I was frustrated. Arif's understanding of fractions as shaded regions over total number of regions convinced him the answer was $5/8$ and kept him from seeing $5/4$ as a possibility. On the other hand, I was delighted. Bob and Arif had just carried on a conversation without me. Each of them took a series of turns addressing one another directly. I started to detect a bit of tension between the two boys, however; we were approaching one of those moments when I had to decide whether we were engaged in an argument of ideas or personalities.

Pili's hand was in the air. She often asked insightful questions. I called on her to ease the tension. Pili said, "I think it is five fourths." This was just what I hoped she would say. I had my hopes set on Pili's reasoning. "Pili, why do you think it is five fourths?" I asked. She said, "Because you said you aren't supposed to add the denominators so I don't think you add them." I responded, "I don't remember if I ever said that, but why does that make sense or why do you think somebody would say that? Could you explain why you wouldn't add those denominators?" Pili shrugged her shoulders and quietly said she did not know why.

My hopes quickly vanished. Pili made no connection to Bob's reasoning and I wondered where she got the idea that I had given her the rule. While I was certainly tempted, I had to remind myself why I had made the choice not to tell students the rule. I wanted Pili and the others to appreciate what it meant to add fractions. This was a nice example of a problem easily solved by following a rule but not easily understood. It was also an interesting problem because the circles and rectangles used to represent the problem could be read as either 5/4 or 5/8.

A Reversal

As lunch time approached, I surveyed the group to see who was thinking what. This information helped in considering what to do the next day. How many people still needed to be convinced the answer was 5/4? As I watched whose hands were raised for which solutions, I was astonished. Moments ago Bob had been arguing for 5/4, but his hand just went up for 5/8. I was so thrown by Bob's change of heart that I did not pay close attention to others' hands. I did notice the group was fairly evenly divided between 5/8 and 5/4, with a few people opting to remain unsure.

I wanted to hear what Bob was thinking. He said, "I think I revise to five eighths. Well, I think it's five eighths because when you have like, a thing like this, and your whole is fourths which is the denominator and five is the numerator which you have to shade in." He turned in his chair and faced students rather than me and continued, "Will someone who thinks that it is five fourths come up here and shade in five out of these four?" (see Figure 7.5). He pointed to a figure I had drawn on the chalkboard earlier. Before I had a chance to call on anyone to respond to Bob's question, he started to explain, "And when you have five eighths, like, o.k. and when you have five eighths, you have eight and then you just have to color in five and you can't do that here because you can't shade in five out of this four." Arif's picture had

FIGURE 7.5: The Figure I Drew Earlier

convinced Bob the answer was 5/8. I had not anticipated revisions might go in this direction. As the bell rang, I decided we had to continue with this same problem the next day.

After the students went to lunch, the classroom teacher and I discussed these events.

> We stood staring at the board, shaking our heads in amazement. This discussion was filled with ideas. The class ended with the unresolved issue of whether 3/4 + 2/4 = 5/4 or 5/8 . . . the difficulty is in their understanding of what the whole is—it occurs to me that maybe Arif and company do not recognize that a solution can be more than one whole. (Heaton journal, 04/16/90)

It made me very nervous when Bob changed his mind, and I questioned whether we were getting anywhere with learning mathematics when people with right answers revised to wrong answers. What was the responsible thing to do? Should I allow students like Bob to be persuaded to revise to a "wrong" answer? I was even beginning to wonder how "wrong" 5/8 was in terms of the representation. Reading the representation as regions shaded in over total number of regions, I could understand Arif's argument that the solution was 5/8.

The Underlying Confusion

There must be some underlying mathematical idea to be understood related to the addition of fractions independent of whether we were considering inches of rain or cups of flour. Unfortunately, Lampert had not observed on these 2 days. I wanted her assistance in understanding both the difficulty we were having and possible ways to respond. Why was it that the same representation could be used to justify two very different solutions? I met with her and explained what students were doing. From her perspective, the difficulty was some mix of students' part–whole interpretation of fractions and the limitations of shaded regions of circles and rectangles as representations of fractions. She reminded me that area models, circles and rectangles with parts shaded, commonly are used as representations when children are first introduced to fractions. Students' part–whole interpretations together with their area representations served to reinforce their solutions. For example, 3/4 + 2/4 could be understood as 5/8 by considering the following representation as five regions shaded out of the total of eight regions (see Figure 7.6). The only way to recognize the representation in Figure 7.6 as 5/4 is to recognize the unit of the fractions being added as fourths.

FIGURE 7.6: Five Regions Shaded Out of Eight Regions

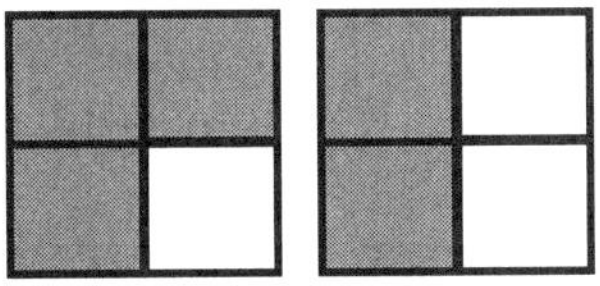

This picture represents five one-fourths or ¼ + ¼ + ¼ + ¼ + ¼. Adding two fractions that are part of a whole divided into fourths should result in more fourths. Students who see the answer in eighths are changing the unit from fourths to eighths. The unit is what gives the fraction meaning, but it is often implicit. There is nothing within this representation that unquestionably defines the unit.

Once Lampert helped me see students' struggles as bigger than inches of rain or cups of flour, I moved away from the idea of switching contexts as a way to help. I wrote in my journal (04/16/90):

> I guess I was surprised that we ended up in the same place with this problem as we did with the rain problem. I thought the confusion was with the unit—because it was an inch—but now I think it is with any unit—because they are confused about the whole—what that means. Whether we are talking about inches or cups of flour, it doesn't matter.

I was not sure what to do. From previous classes, I remembered how persuasive peers could be. Maybe some strong advocates of 5⁄4 would be able to convince those who thought the solution was 5⁄8 to change their minds and do so based on reasoning about the unit.

A Mathematical Argument

The next day, I asked students to figure out the answer, formulate reasons through pictures and words, and then come to some agreement with members of their small groups. I was excited to see students invested in ideas, even if what they were invested in happened to be 5⁄8. I had worked for months to achieve something that resembled a mathematical argument with students. Grappling with the question of whether the solution was 5⁄4 or 5⁄8 was the closest we had come.

I started the whole-class discussion with a survey of hands similar to the one I did at the end of the last class. I noticed Bob was back to thinking 5/4, along with Wu Lee, John, Ana, Luke, Katrina, and Ron, and those that thought 5/8 included Arif, Sipho, Faruq, and Mike. Naruj, alone, held firmly to 1¼ as the only possible solution.

The class discussion evolved into a series of people, including me, trying to communicate points of view we barely understood ourselves. Language, pictures, examples, and counterexamples all become part of the effort. As I heard each response, I had to consider what to do next.

Bob's Conjecture. Bob proposed:

> Well, I was thinking that I challenge everybody that thinks one and one fourth and five fourths because you have one cup and only one cup of flour, not two cups or anything, and so like, say this is one cup, I think it is five eighths, and if this is the only cup that you use because you only have one cup then I think it is five eighths because when you have this, you can do this with one cup, you can shade in five. You can do that [he divided a circle into eight and shaded five, see Figure 7.7]. But you can't do one and one fourth or five fourths with only one [he divided another circle into four]. Because you would have to have two [circles] to get five fourths [see Figure 7.4].

How could I explain to Bob that two wholes or two circles, each divided into fourths, are different than looking at two circles together as one whole, each divided into four to make eighths? How could I explain the importance of the unit and at the same time explain how there could be more than one whole of a particular unit (e.g., two circles) each representing fourths?

FIGURE 7.7: Five Out of Eight Shaded

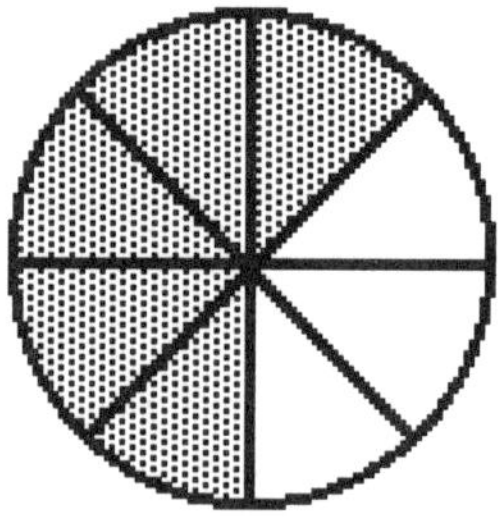

Ana's Conjecture. I asked Ana, who had her hand up, to comment on what Bob said. She immediately disagreed. "I think you can't change the denominator. You are not [pause], can I go up there?" Ana was at a loss for words and wanted to use the chalkboard. As Ana went to the board, Bob responded directly to her, "You are not changing the denominator when you have five eighths. You are not changing it." Several students joined in, "Yes, you are." I hoped Bob did not feel as if people were ganging up on him. I wanted to hear what Ana had to say. I knew from observing that she understood the answer as 5/4. But could she explain it? "Let's see what Ana has to say," I said.

Ana responded to Bob, "You started out with three fourths plus two fourths and now you have got five eighths." Bob admitted, "O.K., Well, yeah, you did change the denominator but let's see you with one, only one cup, make five fourths." I did not want her side-tracked by Bob's challenge. I tried to make space for her to continue. I said, "Let's see what Ana's explanation is. Could you tell us what you are thinking and why?" Ana said, "Well, um, I think, like you can't add two denominators, you can't make these two together and have eight for a denominator." I gently asked, "And why can't you? Why do you think you can't?" I wanted her to find language I felt I lacked.

There was a long pause while Ana stood at the chalkboard and made a few attempts to start talking. Her lips moved but no words came out. She started to draw and then erased what she had drawn. She let out an enormous sigh. I recognized how she might be feeling. I did not know how to explain beyond the rule at this point either. All I could do was reassure her that this was, indeed, a hard question for everyone. I said, "It's tough. It really is hard and you are doing a really good job of trying to think this through."

Arif's Conjecture. I was curious whether this discussion was influencing Arif. We had not heard from him yet that day. I called on him and he said, "I still think it is 5/8 and I have a picture to show." He drew two squares, divided them each into fourths and shaded in three of the four parts in one square and two of the four parts in the other square. Arif explained how he saw that adding 1/4 to 4/4 was adding part of another whole square, which is right as long as the whole square stays divided into fourths no matter how many additional whole squares are used.

At that moment, it occurred to me that comparing the size of 5/8 and 3/4 as they were drawn and labeled here might show that there was less shaded area in something that was 5/8 of a whole circle than in 3/4 of the same whole circle. How could 5/8 be the answer to adding two fractions together when one was $\frac{3}{4}$? Three fourths was larger than $\frac{5}{8}$. I said, "O.K., I have a question. I have seen people draw three fourths and two fourths and come up with this picture of a circle with five eighths shaded (see Figure 7.7). I wonder if you could show me how this picture represents two fourths plus three fourths? Because in addition, this is the total when I add these two pieces together, so could you show me how you could add three fourths and two fourths and get a picture that looks like this?" I struggled with language and groped for words myself.

Mike volunteered to draw a picture to match his conjecture of five eighths. He drew two circles identical to my first example as I posed the question (see Figure 7.4). He said, pointing to the circle on the left, "There is three fourths right there." I asked, "Why isn't that eighths?" He said, "Because this is one, this is one cup of flour and this is another cup of flour and this is two fourths and if you add them together it is just like you have these two cups of flour and there is eight one-fourth spaces of flour and if you, so it is eight and three plus two is five so it would be five eighths." What Mike said was further evidence of the slipperiness of the unit. He said there were eight *one-fourth spaces*, yet concluded the answer was five *eighths*. How could this be?

Scott entertained the possibility of making use of more than one cup. He said, "I could challenge because of what Bob said. Bob said if you, you can't have two cups of flour because it says cup of flour." Bob joined in, "Yeah, cup of flour. That is only one cup." Bob interrupted. I wanted to hear Scott. I said, "And what are you thinking, Scott?" Scott said, "Well, Mike used two cups to get the answer." Bob said, "I know but I only used, on that picture, I only used one because I cut it up into eighths instead of fourths and besides the way I got it with eighths is because with one cup of flour, whoever thinks it is five fourths, with one cup of flour, because it only says cup of flour, five fourths of a cup of flour, then let's see someone draw five out of four." We were back to where we had started—hindered by the part–whole interpretation of fractions. Looking at fourths and eighths in the context of circles and squares was taking us nowhere.

Homework

When I heard the bell ring, all I could think was that maybe the homework, which I always gave on Tuesdays, would make a difference. I assigned students a worksheet of computation on the addition of fractions. They were to find the answer to each problem and draw a picture to support their reasoning. The fractions all had like denominators and added up to less than one. I considered giving them problems in which the answers would be something greater than one, but since I was no longer sure what anyone understood about adding fractions, I stayed with easier problems.

I could afford to spend only one more day on the muffin problem.

> How long is the other teacher (or am I for that matter) going to have patience for this? I think she wonders why I don't just tell them. Sometimes, so do I. Would parents say the same thing? What will the students have found out from their parents about fractions in the process of working on the homework? (Heaton journal, 4/17/90)

How could I help students see that the solution involves two wholes and that some of them were changing the unit? Counting the number of shaded parts and the total number of parts did nothing to define the whole or ensure it would remain constant.

I was not content to leave the problem in a state where we agreed to disagree. Yet, I was not content with just telling students the rule and moving on. Applying rules to get right answers was not the same thing as having reasons for why an answer seemed right. I wrote in my journal before class the next day.

> I want to try to help the students reason why you do not add the denominators without telling them that you don't add them. If I tell them and they don't understand what good is it? It would help them do the problems in the Addison-Wesley textbook and I think that would make both of us feel better. But, would it?

No matter what happened the next day, it would be our last one on this problem for a while. I planned to use the time when we worked on different problems and new topics to learn more about fractions myself, and then try to return to this problem before the school year was over. I was not going to lay this problem to rest until I had reasonable ways to explain to myself and others why the answer was $\frac{5}{4}$.

I arrived at school a bit early the next day to look at homework assignments. I noticed that no one had added the denominators. Everyone had "right" answers. I realized that all of their representations were in the form of circles or rectangles. The only variation was in how the shapes were used. For example, $\frac{1}{4} + \frac{2}{4}$ was represented in either one shape (see Figure 7.7) or two (see Figure 7.6). I decided to start with $\frac{1}{4} + \frac{2}{4}$ and try to move toward $\frac{3}{4} + \frac{2}{4}$.

Whose Understanding Is It?

To begin, I asked someone to share how they thought about $\frac{1}{4} + \frac{2}{4}$. Olivia raised her hand. This was a first! What gave her the confidence to finally speak? Olivia, like several other students in class, entered as a non-English speaker. For the last couple of months, I had noticed her talking in English to people who sat near her. This was the first time she volunteered to speak in math class in front of the whole group. I called on her and she told the group the answer was $\frac{3}{4}$ because "you can't change the denominators." I found myself in a precarious situation. Just about anyone else in the class would be faced with my usual question of why, but in this case I did not want to take the risk of silencing her. Instead, I complimented her response, something I rarely did these days in an effort to remain neutral and accepting of all responses.[1]

Sipho, whose hand was raised while Olivia spoke, relayed a conversation he had with his father the night before.

> Well, last night when I was doing my homework, I was doing a problem that I got stuck on so I asked my dad about the denominators, just like what everybody says about the denominators. As we were talking I just realized that you can never [shakes his head back and forth] add the denominators. Even if it is the same, you still never add them.

I wanted to encourage parental involvement. I could not help but be a bit worried, however, that Sipho's father might not have appreciated the time we were spending on $\frac{3}{4} + \frac{2}{4}$. Sipho explained his understanding of adding fractions.

> Well, if you use two big numbers, real big numbers, and you add the denominators it is going to seem to come out to some big huge number and it wouldn't seem reasonable for a small number at the top and a huge, huge number at the bottom and if you add then it gets too large of a number. What reason would you have to do it like that?

Was Sipho trying to reason about the numerator and denominator as a single quantity or was he talking just about the denominator? If he meant the quantity, could it be he understood that the bigger the denominator, the smaller the quantity? Adding two fractions and getting a bigger number as the denominator (or a smaller fraction) does not make sense. Or, was he thinking of adding just denominators? Sipho was certain one did not add denominators. I was uncertain whether he had a mathematical understanding of why.

David reported on a conversation he had with his father. He drew this on the board (see Figure 7.8). He asked, "Okay, Mike, what is this?" David directed his comment to Mike, who had just announced that when you draw two squares and divide them each into fourths, together you have eight. David moved his finger from one fourth to the next. As he did this, Mike counted fourths, "One fourth, two fourths, three fourths, four fourths." He paused briefly as David moved his finger to the final fourth shaded and announced, "Five eighths." Many of the students, including Mike and David, laughed. It seemed to many students, and perhaps even to Mike, that it made sense the next fraction would be 5/4. I was uncertain why Mike clung to 5/8. David presented a convincing representation, but Mike did not change his mind. I asked David to explain. He said, "One fourth, two fourths, three fourths, four fourths, five fourths. Either that or one and one fourth." Through this exchange, David convinced me he knew that the answer to the muffin problem was 5/4 and could articulate a reason why. His father taught him to count and add on fractions as a way to reason about addition. Was Mike being stubborn or did David's representation really not make sense to him?

Arif announced he also talked with his father. He shared what his father told him. "It would equal one and one fourth, but then I asked if it was five eighths or five fourths. First, he thought five eighths and then he said it was five fourths. It is just like David said [Arif counted the fourths on his fingers] one fourth, two fourths, three fourths, four fourths, five fourths."

I faced new issues. Were students' explanations reflective of their own understandings or their parents'? How was a parent's authority any different than the authority of the teacher or the textbook when it came to the "telling" of mathematical knowledge? I was teaching students to think of themselves as authorities for what made sense. Did that mean they should question the authority of their parents? How could I show respect for parents' ideas yet at the same time push stu-

FIGURE 7.8: David's Drawing

dents to understand mathematics in ways their parents never experienced?

The bell rang. I told students of my plans to move on to something else the next day. It seemed that many of them had the idea that the denominators were not to be added together. I wanted to push harder on reasons why. I suggested they might want to think this through with their parents again. David, who I thought learned a reason from his father for thinking 5/4, made a striking remark. He said, "I think I know what the answer is but I just don't know whether or not to change the denominator. I think it is five fourths." Even though David thought the answer was five fourths, and his father had a reason, he apparently still did not feel like *he* had a reason.

A Need to Understand Why

After class I wrote in my journal:

> I was surprised that students were still engaged in the discussion even after some of them were told by their parents not to add the denominators. Figuring out *why* was truly the focus. (Heaton journal, 04/18/90)

I needed to get a better grip on this math problem myself before we continued. I finally felt like I had a real mathematical question that came from students and intrigued me. In my journal, I wrote about my decision to stick with one topic over time and the benefits of this way of thinking about curriculum.

> This is truly an intriguing problem to me. I think we got as far as we did because of the intensity of the discussion over the last few days. I think if I had dropped it and tried to pick it up at a later date the outcome may have been different. I think there is something about what has been building over the last few days. Two problems in four days—this is a first for me. It was clear that some students had discussed the problem at home. Would this have happened if they had not been given homework dealing with fractions?

During the next 6 weeks, I went on to other mathematical topics. I promised myself to return to fractions, specifically this problem, before the school year ended. In the meantime, I wanted to consider alternative representations, or figure out a way to construct an argument for the correct solution with the representations the students had been using.

RETURN TO THE PROBLEM: SIX WEEKS LATER

It was the first week of June and there were only two math classes left in the school year. We had returned to the topic of fractions and I was committed to finding a way to return to $3/4 + 2/4$. Most recently, I had introduced students to folding paper strips to represent different fractions and compare sizes. When students folded strips, some just moved the folds in the strip around until the parts were even. Others used a ruler first, divided the length of the strip into equal parts, marked where the folds ought to go, and then folded the strip. Some students were challenged when I asked them to divide a paper strip that was a bit longer than 9 inches into thirds. Some students used rulers and folded back the portion of the strip that was greater than 9 inches so that each third would come out an even 3 inches long. I wrote in my journal (05/31/90) after the class:

> Ron took a ruler and measured the strip—9½ inches. He turned back the excess and divided nine by three. I thought he gave a great explanation why he did it. It was too messy. He wanted to get the work done. He wanted it to turn out even . . . I asked people to respond to Ron. Ana said, "I don't think he can do that. You can't change the whole." This *is* the point. This is one of those statements that people might think you paid or planted a child to say. It was wonderful.

I told students folding back part of the strip and not using it was changing the size of the whole. To follow up on this idea, I gave each student an 8-inch strip of yellow paper and asked them, for homework, to try to divide it into tenths and write about how they did it. I wanted to begin the next class with a discussion of what they had done. I had been waiting and watching for an opportune time to reconnect to $3/4 + 2/4$.

I decided that in the second part of the next class, I would give students paper strips and ask them to show their solutions to $3/4 + 2/4$. I thought they would fold two strips and shade them to look like Figure 7.9. I wrote the following in my notes as the plan for the next math class:

FIGURE 7.9: 3/4 + 2/4 with Paper Strips

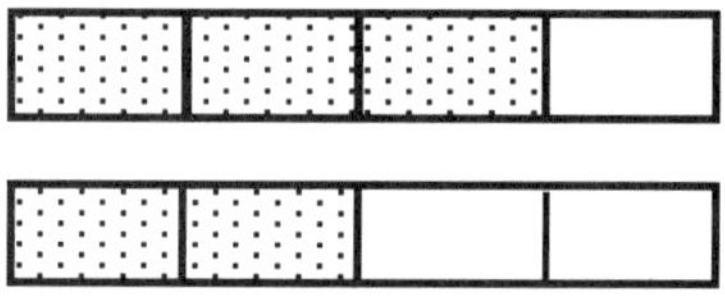

1. What did you do with the yellow strips?
   Were you able to make tenths out of an 8-inch strip?
   If so, how?
   If not, why not?
2. Is there a way to use paper strips to show $\frac{3}{4} + \frac{2}{4}$?
   If so, how?
   If not, why not?
   How many fourths are in one whole?

When the class began, students took out their yellow strips of paper and talked about ways they found to divide the strip into 10 equal pieces. Some had folded the paper, others had measured. I was eager to move on to $\frac{3}{4} + \frac{2}{4}$.

Students put away the yellow strips and took out two of the white paper strips we used in class the day before. I reintroduced the problem of $\frac{3}{4} + \frac{2}{4}$. I was prepared to hear moans and groans of fourth-grade students being asked to reconsider something they thought they had finished and put to rest long ago. This was not the case. There were no signs of resistance. It appeared I was not the only one who still cared about this question. I told students to use paper strips to explain their solutions.

Students immediately started talking with one another about the problem. I stood back and watched. I felt no need to direct their talk or provide any additional structure to the task. Students seemed intrigued and invested in figuring out how to use paper strips to represent their thinking. There was a life within these small groups that I witnessed on only a few other occasions. With 15 minutes remaining in class, I began a whole-group discussion, even though it looked as if students could continue talking among themselves for much longer.

A New Way of Seeing

Luke was on his knees, almost on top of his desk with his hand in the air, when I asked for someone to begin. "I think it is five fourths," he said. I asked, "And do you have a way to talk about it?" Luke started with, "My dad . . . " I abruptly interrupted. I wanted to discourage an appeal to outside authorities. I reminded Luke of the paper strips. "Do you have a way to talk about it with paper strips?" Luke was willing to put aside his father's ideas and talk about his own. He made the same configuration I had hoped for. "I took two strips. One with two fourths colored. I made four pieces out of one and four pieces out of the other. I colored in two for two fourths. I colored in three to make three fourths on the other strip [see Figure 7.9]. I added the colored in ones, two plus three is five. And when you have two denominators that are the same, adding one fraction to another fraction, you do not add the denominators."

Luke had slipped into the rule. I wanted students to reason about denominators with paper strips without using rules. I asked, again, "O.K., how can you make sense of that with paper strips? What does the four in the denominator have to do with those paper strips?" Luke said, "They show you how many pieces you are supposed to divide it into." I replaced his "it" with the word *whole* and repeated what he had said, "They show you how many pieces you are supposed to divide the whole into." I was trying to emphasize the connection between the fourths the strip was divided into and fourths as a unit of the whole.

I asked, "O.K., does someone want to comment or add to Luke's idea?" I was curious what Arif, who earlier had been the leading proponent for $5/8$, was thinking. He said, "Well, I am not sure but I think I agree with Luke, one and one fourth. But, I think five fourths and one and one fourth are the same. I am not sure about five eighths." A few students shot their hands up in the air and started gasping in ways that interrupted Arif. I asked the students to let him finish. Arif continued, "Well, I like, I had four fourths and that was one whole and then like I added another strip just like Luke did. I got like one and one fourth but there were eight parts in all of the strips that we used, there were eight parts." I tried to say back to Arif what I thought he had said: "So you think five fourths is the same as one and one fourth but then you are wondering about this five eighths." Arif added, "They might all be the same." Arif had reasons for thinking $5/4$ and $1\,1/4$ and yet he did not seem convinced to abandon the possibility of $5/8$.

A New Way of Being

I had watched Lampert teach fifth graders all year and been paying attention to how she responded to students' ideas. She repeated or paraphrased what she heard students say and in doing so added or replaced words in minor ways to alter meaning. Her changes were subtle but substantive. They pushed the mathematical ideas by building on the ideas of students in the direction of the mathematics she intended to teach. It seemed like a way to work with the students' ideas that was responsive to students as well as to the mathematics she wanted to teach.

I called on Ana. "What do you think?" She said, "I think it is five fourths or one and one fourth." Rather than have her explain why she thought these were solutions, I hoped she might be able to help Arif and so I asked, "And why not five eighths?" She responded, "Because you are adding two fourths and three fourths. And when you do, this would be one whole and this would a little bit bigger." I tried to say what I thought she meant to say: "It sounds like when you are adding two fourths plus three fourths you are getting something bigger than the whole. Are you getting something longer than one paper strip?" Ana nodded in agreement. If we could talk about the solution as being something more than one paper strip, I thought it might help students see the answer as greater than one whole.

It also seemed like one way to address Bob's issue of long ago that the answer could only be in terms of one whole, *an* inch or *a* cup of flour. I wondered what he thought now. I called on him. He said, "I think it is five fourths. Four fourths equals a whole. Since it is four fourths and that is your whole and then you have one more fourth. Five fourths is one fourth more than your whole." Two paper strips, each divided into fourths, gave a way to visualize the answer as more than one whole, as some number of fourths more than four fourths or the length of one paper strip, one whole.

Naruj caught my eye. He said, "I don't think five eighths should be up there because when I look on my paper, one whole is much bigger than five eighths and I don't think that five eighths should be there." I noticed he had two paper strips in his hands and said, "You made up two strips here. Can I hold these up?" I held up his paper strips (see Figure 7.10). I continued to talk, "You have one divided into fourths and one divided into eighths. I am going to fold it back to where he has up to here is five eighths and here is the whole. What do you think about that? Naruj, would you tell them again why you don't think it could be five eighths?" Naruj responded, "Because five eighths is smaller than three fourths or a whole. Because it says three fourths plus two fourths so I don't think it can be one of the numbers." I repeated what I thought Naruj was saying: "So, you are saying one of the numbers is three fourths and you are adding something to it so it is going to be bigger than three fourths but here when you look at these two

FIGURE 7.10: Comparing 5/8 and 3/4 with Paper Strips

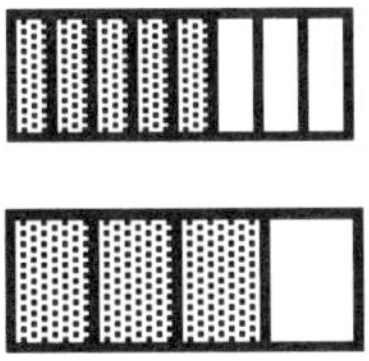

strips, three fourths, all by itself, without adding anything to it, is bigger than five eighths. What do other people think?" The bell rang. I wished we had more time. It seemed as if we were finally getting somewhere. Students were beginning to compare the size of fractions. They also seemed to be trying to wrap their minds around why the unit was fourths not eighths and the solution was more than one whole. This was reasoning I was still struggling to see clearly.

NOTE

1. This decision represented a dilemma for me. While this move may have helped Olivia's confidence, it is problematic and exemplifies the kind of subtle inequities in classroom interaction that happen in relation to gender. What message am I sending to Olivia by not expecting the same from her as I do from other students? Am I doing a disservice to females by acquiescing to their shyness and not pushing them for fear of embarrassing them? Besides this interaction with Olivia, I had other gender concerns. Why were many of the classroom interactions that resembled discussions dominated by just a few students, and a majority of the time, a handful of males? Was I naively promoting inequity? These are important questions that are outside the scope of this study but deserve a book of their own.

CHAPTER 8

Learning to See Knowledge Differently

Since that year of teaching, when someone asks what my math teaching experiences in fourth grade were like, I often have relayed the series of lessons described in Chapter 7 and my struggles with the question of what to do next as an example of what I was learning about learning mathematics for understanding. The math problem, $\frac{2}{4} + \frac{3}{4}$, is a powerful example for me because I can use my understanding of it over time to trace and explain how my conceptions about mathematics and teaching have changed.

PRIOR CONCEPTIONS OF MATHEMATICS AND TEACHING

In my past experiences, teaching students how to find the solution to a problem like $\frac{3}{4} + \frac{2}{4}$ would not have been difficult. I would have told students the rule for adding two fractions with like denominators—add the numerators, keep the denominators the same—and they would have applied it to numerous calculations. Addition of fractions would be mastered in several days. My challenge was to find ways to help students to memorize not only this rule but the other rules that governed operations on fractions and whole numbers and to develop strategies for storing and recalling the rules as needed. Students did not have to understand why rules made sense, only how they worked to produce a right answer.

Students were learning procedural knowledge consistent with my conception of mathematics at the time. Hiebert and Lefevre (1986) define procedural knowledge as having two parts, "knowledge of symbols and syntax and knowledge of rules, algorithms, or procedures used to solve mathematical tasks" (p. 6). The procedures are hierarchically organized and stored in textbooks as a fixed body of knowledge. Jackson

(1986) describes it as knowledge that "can be 'passed' from one person to another or from one text to a person; thus we can see it as 'detachable' from persons . . . preserved in books . . . it can be forgotten by those who once knew it" (p. 118). You either know something or you don't. He describes the teaching that accompanies this view of knowledge as teaching in the mimetic tradition. Mimetic teaching "gives a central place to the transmission of factual and procedural knowledge from one person to another, through an essentially imitative process" (p. 117). It is knowledge that is easily assessed and offers a certainty to questions of purpose and progress in teaching and learning.

> It can be judged right or wrong, accurate or inaccurate, correct or incorrect on the basis of a comparison with the teacher's own knowledge or with some other model as found in a textbook or other instructional material. Not only do judgments of this sort yield a measure of the success of teaching within this tradition, they also are the chief criterion by which learning is measured. (Jackson, 1986, p. 118)

This description matches my views of mathematical knowledge before learning about the reforms in math education. I talked about my views with Reineke in my initial interview with him before this school year began. At the time of this interview, I had been in graduate school for a full year, the year in which I was introduced to the reforms in mathematics education.

> *Reineke:* Has your thinking on what it means to know something mathematically changed since you were last in the classroom? [a year earlier]
>
> *Heaton:* Yes.
>
> *Reineke:* Can you describe that change?
>
> *Heaton:* In the past, to know division would be for a child to be able to do the computation, get the right answer and not have to explain how they did it: I mean what's really happening with those numbers, and not just the steps that they have to do to get the answer. Another thing that has changed is probably the amount of reasoning that I would ask kids to do to explain how they come up with an answer. In the past, I would have been looking for the right answer and probably wouldn't have asked them very often how they got the answer.
>
> (Reineke interview, 08/89)

CHANGING CONCEPTIONS OF MATHEMATICS AND TEACHING

In the series of lessons described in Chapter 7, I was not content to teach students to solve the problem of $3/4 + 2/4$ the way I would have done in the past, but I was unsure just what was important to learn. What was there besides rules for students to know? On what conceptual mathematical ideas was this rule based? Why and how did the rule work? There had to be some underlying mathematical meaning for these rules. At the time, these were meanings I did not understand.

In this series of lessons, I was struggling between two different conceptions of mathematical knowledge—loosening my hold on rules and procedures, while searching for some deeper conceptual meaning. Being uncertain was unsettling. I knew a way to stop mucking about with the addition of fractions and move on. I could teach students the rule, have them practice it until they were proficient at getting right answers, and go on to the next topic. This was what I would have done before this year. In the midst of the mess I felt like I was in, the certainty of that view of mathematics and teaching practice appealed to me. If I thought about mathematical knowledge as something constructed, however, I could not so easily deal with the question of what to do next. Learning a rule for how to add fractions was not my ultimate goal. There had to be more to this. But what? If reasoning was what I was after, students who were thinking $5/8$ had thoughtful explanations for why they thought so. Was I to value their reasons even if they supported a wrong solution? I did not know how to push students' reasoning to help them see the solution was $5/4$ and not $5/8$. I could not identify what made the difference, especially when I looked at the reasonableness of either solution as represented by the area models (see Figure 7.6).

My struggles with my own conception of mathematics throughout that set of lessons are related to my questions of how to proceed in the classroom. I wanted what students were learning about mathematics to be different, but I did not quite know what it was that they should be learning. I had already figured out the answer was not to be found in the teacher's guide. Throughout this series of lessons, I made decisions about what to do next based on my best guess at the time about what was going on with students' understandings of the mathematics, as I struggled to figure out what it was I wanted them to learn.

The Concept, Not the Context

Between the day I gave the rain problem and planned to give the muffin problem, I assumed the use of rulers prompted by the context of measuring inches of rain was the main difficulty. I wanted to get as far away from linear measurement as possible. After switching contexts from inches of rain to cups of flour and seeing what students did with the muffin problem, I realized the mathematics that students were grappling with was not something resolved by attending to flour rather than rain. The difficulty was with shifting units and it did not matter whether the context was rain or flour.

The irony to this sequence of events and my decision about what to do next was that it was probably counter to what others might have done who have a deeper mathematical understanding of the difficulty students faced. Pushing students to consider addition of fractions in the context of linear measurement might have been quite useful. "A number line can be used to model rational numbers greater than one (mixed numbers) provided the child already understands certain basic concepts about fractions before starting the number line" (Behr & Post, 1988, p. 221). Each fraction on the number line represents a distance. The interpretation of addition is finding the sum of two distances (Behr & Post, 1988). One can locate the distance ¾ on the number line and add a distance of 2⁄4 to it (see Figure 8.1). The solution, 5⁄4, also can be thought of as the iteration of the unit fraction, ¼, five times.

Helping Each Other See

Once I figured out that students' difficulty with adding fractions was something other than rain or flour, I gave up on the idea of switching contexts. I stayed with the muffin problem over several days but was at a loss for how to push students' thinking on it. I hoped students would push one another. "Interacting with classmates helps children

FIGURE 8.1: 3/4 + 2/4 Represented on a Number Line

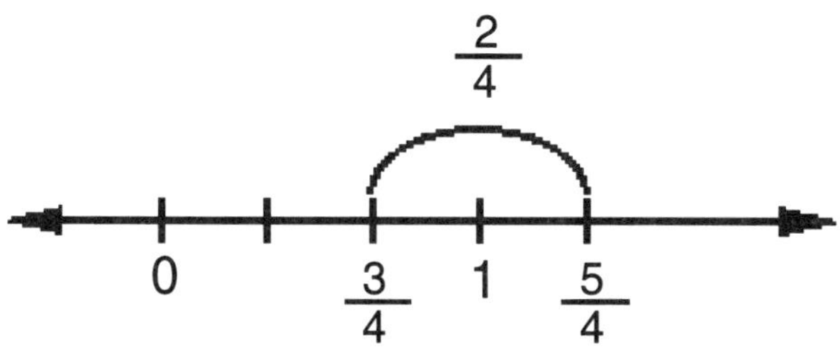

construct knowledge, learn other ways to think about ideas, and clarify their own thinking" (NCTM, 1989, p. 26). When I hoped students would help one another see, I did not consider that they might persuade one another to see $\frac{5}{8}$ as the solution. I was unprepared for this.

I was at a loss for what to do with their ideas and I did not know what kind of problem to give them if I moved away from the muffin problem. Why was this such a hard thing to articulate? What Ana tried to communicate was the need to hold the unit constant when adding two fractions; to see the answer as $\frac{5}{8}$ means a change in the unit. I was not as clear then as I am now how the area representations reinforced this idea and made it difficult to explain the differences in how students were thinking of the unit. I felt like the problem of trying to explain the issue of the unit with students' representations pushed at the limits of understanding for anyone who thought the solution was $\frac{5}{4}$, including myself. In the situation, I looked to students as resources. I hoped they could help each other because I did not have an articulated sense of the mathematical terrain into which we had ventured.

Homework

My lack of understanding about the mathematical terrain, and how tasks could move students into or out of certain parts of it, is something I learned through the homework assignment I gave. The homework did not go as I had planned. Students got plenty of practice with right answers by adding fractions that totaled less than one, but the problems I gave them did not push them into the same mathematical territory as the fractions totaling more than one. The part–whole interpretation and the circular and rectangular representations they knew so well worked without a hitch for all of these problems. I did not realize this until I had a stack of papers with all right answers in my hands. As I look back on this now, I am not certain just what difference I was hoping homework would make. Perhaps a part of me hoped just doing the computation, repeatedly, would somehow lead to understanding, and drawing pictures would be some additional guarantee that something was learned.

A New Representation

Area models of the circles and rectangles were problematic because they represented a part–whole interpretation of fractions and there was nothing to clearly identify the whole. Understanding the differences in the interpretation of these representations as $\frac{5}{8}$ or $\frac{5}{4}$ hinges on understanding what the unit is, as well as understanding the interpretation of fractions as shaded areas within circles and rectangles.

I was excited when we returned to the problem of $\frac{3}{4} + \frac{2}{4}$ near the end of the school year. The paper strips seemed useful. However, since then I have come to realize that those paper strips really fall into the same family of representations as circles and rectangles. They are all area models and all involve partitioning a whole into equal parts. What I think was somewhat different with the paper strips was my saying, "Shade five one-fourth parts," a phrase that makes the whole—fourths—explicit.

When we were using circles and rectangles, we were all talking about fractions as wholes and parts that were shaded. For example, Bob's initial argument for why the solution could not be $\frac{5}{4}$ was, "Will someone who thinks that it is $\frac{5}{4}$ come up here and shade in five out of these four?" Six weeks later, Bob was thinking differently about fractions: "Five fourths is one fourth more than your whole." Students, like Bob, who could now see that the solution was $\frac{5}{4}$ appeared to understand that five one-fourth parts covered more area than one whole unit and required the use of a second unit region (Behr & Post, 1988). "Five one-fourth parts" offered a different mathematical conception of $\frac{5}{4}$ than "five shaded out of four." As a result of this awareness of the whole, some students had a new understanding about why the solution was $\frac{5}{4}$ and not $\frac{5}{8}$, since $\frac{5}{8}$ would be less than one whole. They were learning some subtle, important variations and distinctions in the meaning of fractions that enabled them to see new things.

NEW CONCEPTIONS OF MATHEMATICS AND TEACHING

Since teaching that lesson, I have explored the mathematical terrain related to the problem of $\frac{3}{4} + \frac{2}{4}$. One of the ways I pursued my interest was to delve into research in math education on the topic of fractions. Fractions are known for the difficulty they cause students (Behr, Lesh, Post, & Silver, 1983) and teachers (Post, Behr, & Lesh, 1988).

Multiple Interpretations and Representations

Some researchers argue that the difficulty stems from the multiple interpretations of rational numbers (Behr et al., 1983). These authors note as many as six different interpretations of fractions, including "a part-to-whole comparison, a decimal, a ratio, an indicated division (quotient), an operator, and a measure of continuous or discrete quantities"

(p. 93). Rational numbers are also part of the larger mathematical category called multiplicative structures, described and analyzed in relationship to addition in the context of whole numbers (see Chapter 4). Children bring whole number understanding embedded in additive structures to fractions. I draw on an example used by Behr and Post (1988), using the fraction $3/5$.

> There are at least two important relationships between 3 and 5; one is additive, the other is multiplicative. The additive relationship between 5 and 3 is what the child already knows; it is expressed by the difference between 5 and 3—2. The multiplicative relationship is something the child doesn't know, and this relationship is essential to understanding that $3/5$ is a single number, that it has a size, and what the size actually is. (p. 196)

Why try to understand fractions as single numbers? When students add $3/4 + 2/4$ and get $5/8$, do they see each of $3/4$ and $2/4$ as one or two numbers (Behr & Post, 1988)? Do they have an understanding of "three fourths" or do they see this as the whole number three over the whole number four? Bob's initial interpretation of five parts shaded out of four was more like seeing $5/4$ as two whole numbers, while the view of $5/4$ as five one-fourth parts seems more like understanding $5/4$ as a number, a quantity.

In my study of fractions, I came across several ways of interpreting the problem $3/4 + 2/4$ that would make the solution $5/8$ reasonable. For example, suppose in playing softball Susie gets three hits in four times up to bat. This can be written as three hits out of four times at the bat or $3/4$. The next time Susie gets two hits in four times, or $2/4$. What Susie did altogether is like $3/4 + 2/4$ or $5/8$. The total number of hits is placed over the number of times at bat. In the context of batting averages, these fractions are ratios. Adding ratios is not the same as adding quantities.

A second way to justify the solution $5/8$ is by saying that two fourths of one plus three fourths of one is five eighths of two. Consider the following scenario. Johnny has a cake that is cut into four pieces. He eats two of them. Mary has the same size cake and cuts it into four pieces. She eats three of them. How much cake have they eaten all together? They have eaten one and one fourth pieces of one cake. The difficulty with this solution is that it was necessary to have two cakes to start with in order for the second person to get three pieces. Even if the cakes happen to be the same size, they can easily be conceived of as different units or wholes.

A Historical Context

My study of fractions also led me into the history of rational numbers. I was led there through a mathematician friend's interpretation of the difficulty students had with adding fractions. He drew connections between students' struggles and the history of fractions.

> You know you're trying to teach them addition after all and not just ways of putting fractions together. You have to think, how did addition start historically? How did fractions first get added? They weren't always added. I mean people, Greeks, did not like to do arithmetic of any sort with fractions. They felt just like our kids. They hated them. The fractions were ratios. I mean you should read what they wrote about arithmetic with ratios, how they thought of it. They drew lines and said well it's all measurement with numbers. I mean they started to think about measurements. There is no way to add fractions without thinking of them as measurement. . . . So I guess with little kids you would have to think culturally, one has to think culturally about how things do progress. (personal communication, 05/17/90)

Culturally, how did the idea of fractions progress? I have selected several of the particulars of the history of fractions to include here. "Most of the ancient theory of fractions centered about the concept of ratio" (Smith, 1958, p. 210). The Egyptians and the Babylonians were the first two civilizations to contribute to our present-day understanding of mathematics (Kline, 1972). Both of these cultures used mathematics to answer questions that arose for them in their daily lives. The Egyptians, for example, wanted a means of being more precise in their measurement of quantities—length, weight, and time. Thus arose the need and development of the concept of a fraction in the context of measurement (Scott, 1969; Smith, 1958), for "seldom will a length appear to contain an exact number of linear units" (Eves, 1969, p. 58). Think back to what Ron did with his paper strip when he tried to divide a strip longer than 9 inches into thirds—he turned back the portion of the strip that was greater than nine. His reason for not dealing with the extra was that it was too messy. The Egyptians invented fractions to deal with that extra he folded back.

While historical "facts" associated with fractions or the particulars of the mathematical history of fractions may be interesting, there is something more important that a study of the history of mathematics represents. It has been a powerful means of seeing mathematical knowledge as constructed and developed by humans, in a social and cultural context. Arcavi, Bruckheimer, and Bens-zvi (1987) discuss the benefits of looking historically at mathematics.

> The historical context may foster the creation of a reasonable image of mathematics and mathematical activity as a human, creative, and dynamic endeavor, as opposed to the more common view of mathematics dropping "ready-made-from-the-skies." (p. 19)

Mathematical knowledge is a human construction (Kitcher, 1984). This is an idea I was only beginning to understand and experience with children.

The possible interpretations and representations of fractions are numerous and vary in ways that lead to subtle and not so subtle differences in meaning. There is no such thing as the perfect representation.

> Since there are no single most powerful forms of representation, the teacher must have at hand a veritable armamentarium of alternative forms of representation, some of which derive from research whereas others originate in the wisdom of practice. (Shulman, 1986, p. 9)

Choosing the appropriate representation means weighing its strengths and limitations for representing an idea, at a given moment, with a given group of students. And then, what one person may be able to see in the representation may not be visible to someone else.

This study of rational numbers has pushed me to begin to see multiple ways to construct, interpret, represent, and communicate the meaning of mathematical ideas. It happens in classrooms among teachers and students, in universities among mathematicians, and in the field of math education among researchers. Understanding an area of mathematics is ongoing work. Fractions, rational numbers, and multiplicative structures are areas of mathematics whose complexity of meaning continues to be explored by people who continue to learn new things. Fuson (1988) notes how as a community of math education researchers "we have not been able to agree on a single way to structure these conceptual fields, either for multiplication or rational number situations" (p. 260). These are complex mathematical ideas, a terrain of deep uncertain, unsettled mathematical issues. Hiebert and Behr (1988), editors of *Number Concepts and Operations in the Middle Grades*, remind their readers of the tentativeness of knowledge and that even knowledge that seems certain is subject to change.

> But we must remember that theories always are tentative and sometimes wrong. They can never be cast in stone. They must be treated as working hypotheses, tested and refined and tested again. It is only through the cyclical process of building and testing theories that significant progress can be made. (p. 16)

As I look back on my initial interview with Reineke, before I started teaching that year, I am surprised by my view of mathematical knowledge and how I thought I was going to go about learning what I did not know. I started the year thinking that I did not know enough mathematics. Reineke asked me how I planned to deal with this.

> I think the hurdle of my own knowledge of mathematics—I don't feel like that's something I've been able to do ahead of time, that it's not possible for me to learn everything I need to know about mathematics before I teach this. And that I have to deal with it as it comes up and figure out what it is I don't know and try to learn more about it. (interview, 08/89).

Years later, I agree that my ongoing work as a teacher is to figure out what it is that I don't know and learn more about it. The difference now is that I have a new appreciation for what I do and do not understand. And *not knowing*, at this point in my work as a teacher, is not a shortcoming. Knowing what I don't know and having an interest in and means for investigating what I don't know, is what keeps me developing as a teacher. Moreover, it is what keeps me growing as a person.

LEARNING THE RIVER

I knew there was some mathematics that I did not know. I knew there was a mathematical territory with which I was unfamiliar. I knew there was a terrain or aspects of a terrain I could learn. I have learned some particulars of the terrain as well as how knowledge about the terrain is constructed. The way I learned about the terrain was to go exploring in it myself. I return to images of navigating a river to consider how a sense of the terrain helps one navigate through it. George Byron Merrick (1987) in *Old Times on the Upper Mississippi* reflects on the knowledge of riverboat pilots during Twain's time on the river.

> The pilot of that day was absolutely dependent upon his knowledge of and familiarity with the natural landmarks on either bank of the river for

> guidance in working his way through and over the innumerable sand-bars and crossings. (p. 78)

Navigation demands learning the river in ways that help one move about easily, no matter what one encounters. Merrick (1987) writes:

> To "know the river" under those conditions meant to know absolutely the outline of every range of bluffs and hills, as well as every isolated knob or even tree-top. It meant that the man at the wheel must know these outlines absolutely, under the constantly changing point of view of the moving steamer; so that he might confidently point his steamer at a solid wall of blackness, and guided only by the shape of distant hills, and by the mental picture which he had of them, know the exact moment at which to put his wheel over and sheer his boat away from an impending bank. (p. 79)

There is a paradox here about knowledge and knowing. How can a pilot ever know the river absolutely—if his point of view is constantly changing and the river is ever-changing? Doesn't this mean that we need to reconsider what it means to *know* something? What Twain tried to learn, the river, is something that can never, given its nature, be entirely known.

Many times on the river Twain thought he had learned the river or that he could know everything necessary for navigation—once and for all he thought he had learned the river. At one point, he even tried to make a list of what he had learned under the assumption that he had finally completed his education. Twain writes:

> When I had learned the name and position of every visible feature of the river; when I had so mastered its shape that I could shut my eyes and trace it from St. Louis to New Orleans; when I had learned to read the face of the water as one would cull the news from the morning paper; and finally, when I had trained my dull memory to treasure up an endless array of sounding and cross-marks, and keep fast hold of them, I judged my education was complete: so I got to tilting my cap to the side of my head, and wearing a toothpick in my mouth at the wheel. (Twain, 1883/1990, p. 67)

It was not too long before Mr. Bixby asked him a question about the river for which he did not have an answer. Twain addressed Mr. Bixby, "But what I want to know is, if I have got to keep up an everlasting measuring of the banks of this river, twelve hundred miles, month in and month out?" (p. 69). To which Mr. Bixby replied, "Of course."

The same infinity of the task that Twain found with learning to navigate the river applies to what I have learned about the nature of learning mathematics and learning to teach mathematics for understanding. Learning is inherent to the work. The account of my learning I offer here is unique. Like Twain, this was my first time on the river. Next time I will know from the start that "the whole river is bristling with exigencies in a moment" (Twain, 1883/1990, p. 92). And, given what I have learned from this first journey and my study of it in the years since, I will be prepared.

CONCLUSION

Learning to Teach While Inventing a Practice

Through efforts to enact my vision of mathematics teaching, that vision itself was revised and reconstructed. I found I needed to simultaneously change, teach, learn, and develop the very thing I was learning. For example, to begin to facilitate productive discussions, I had to develop concrete particulars about what might count as "productive" while the discussion was happening, and how to make such productivity possible on a moment-to-moment basis. I learned that initiating a mathematical discussion is dependent on having interesting mathematical ideas to discuss. What counts as an "interesting mathematical idea" is, in part, situation-specific. I also was learning that there was more to sustaining a discussion than merely asking students questions repeatedly. As the teacher, it was my responsibility to *do* something with students' ideas. My ability to help students construct their own understandings of mathematical ideas was connected to what I understood about the mathematics as well as my capacity to hear and interpret students' understandings. Pedagogical skills and mathematical knowledge are interconnected and continually constructed and reconstructed in the course of teaching.

Continuous invention of a practice is inherent to the work of teaching mathematics for understanding. Even teachers perceived by some as "experts" must invent a practice of teaching as they work (e.g., Ball, 1993a, 1993b; Lampert, 1986, 1990). Teaching mathematics for understanding is not something that is ever completely learned. One can get better at it but the "it," the teaching, is forever under construction.

THE LOGIC AND LIMITS OF INVENTION

To say the new way of teaching mathematics that I was trying to enact was one based on ideas of invention evokes helpful images. The metaphor is useful, however, only as long as the grounds on which I make connections, as well as the limits of any applications I intend, are understood.

Why Invention?

Several factors underlie the argument that learning to teach mathematics for understanding must be understood as entailing invention as well as learning. First of all, the vision of mathematics teaching offered by the reform documents is underdetermined. This point is supported whether one looks at different policy documents representing the reforms in mathematics education or at the work of mathematics education researchers whose perspectives on teaching are based on their studies of students' learning.

Policy documents offer fairly clear visions of mathematical knowledge and theories of learning, but are less clear about details of a practice of teaching rooted in these ideas about knowledge and learning. Some mathematics education researchers, through studying students' learning, have reached similar conclusions with regard to the lack of a single way to teach. For example, researchers who have done extensive study of children's understandings of addition and subtraction as part of Cognitively Guided Instruction (Carpenter & Fennema, 1988) have considered how to use knowledge of children's cognitions in teaching in ways that are responsive to students yet do not prescribe practice. A similar perspective underlies the work of Yackel, Cobb, and Wood (1991) and Yackel and Cobb (1996), researchers in classrooms where teachers are trying to teach mathematics in conceptual ways. They note the nature of interactions in these classrooms: "We speak not only of the negotiation of norms but their continual renegotiation" (Yackel et al., 1991, p. 397). Thus, teaching entails a continuous negotiation of moves determined by the situation rather than defined and prescribed in advance.

A second reason why it makes sense to view the process of teacher change as entailing invention is that this kind of teaching of mathematics is so fundamentally dependent on being responsive to students. Of course, one can learn how to anticipate what students might say. One can increase one's ability to predict what might happen. One can even learn to think through possible responses. But all this would still be insufficient to plan exactly what will happen or how one might respond in any given moment of teaching. This makes the teaching of mathematics for understanding itself unpredictable, uncertain, subject to surprises, and requiring improvisation.

A third reason why the idea of inventing a practice is reasonable centers on the nature of what it means to know and come to know the content being taught. It matters that what is being learned is mathematics and that the view of mathematical knowledge underlying these reforms is a constructivist one. Both what mathematics gets learned and how it gets learned are strongly determined by social interaction, which cannot be prescribed. One learns mathematics in a community through efforts to simultaneously create and communicate a plausible argument, an argument invented in practice.

The Limits of Invention

The metaphor of invention helps to reveal the compositional process of teaching and learning to teach that otherwise might go unnoticed. It also, through its seductiveness, may obscure understanding. On the one hand, inventing a practice of teaching mathematics while teaching mathematics implies no rehearsal for the work of teaching. That is, one cannot rehearse the execution of a set of preplanned decisions and moves. But as stated above, there are certain things, like anticipating what students might say or do in the context of a particular math problem, for example, that *can* be learned outside the situation. Such learnings might help in anticipating how to act or teach in the situation. Learning to figure out what needs to be considered to make crucial decisions about what to do next during the act of teaching is central to this work. On the other hand, one must not assume mistakenly that this means there is nothing teachers can learn. Quite the contrary. Later in the chapter, I will return to the topic of teacher education. The image of inventing a practice of teaching also could suggest mistakenly that all practice is equal, that there are not better or worse ways of working, that there are no standards of quality or worth. As is common when developing criteria for assessing a new practice, it is often easier to articulate what is not acceptable rather than what is. While standards for good practice remain ill defined, judgment is both possible and necessary.

EXPECTATIONS OF DRAMATIC CHANGES

I did not enter this year of teaching expecting that what I needed to learn to do was invent a practice. Rather, I expected I was learning to implement a way of teaching radically different from the teaching I had done in the past, a way that was itself defined and articulated. My task, or so I imagined, was, in time and with experience, to learn to do it.

I expected the changes to be dramatic ones. Images of the changes

I thought necessary are arrayed below, alongside patterns central to my former practice.

A: Old Practice of Teaching Mathematics	B: Goal—Teaching Mathematics for Understanding
Teachers tell.	Teachers do not tell.
Teachers follow a prescribed curriculum.	Teachers do not follow a prescribed curriculum.
Math problems have a single right answer.	Math problems have no single right answer.
Students always work alone to do math.	Students do not work alone to do math.

To envision change in terms of extreme behavioral dichotomies is not unusual. Dieters, seeking new svelteness, do it when they resolve to eliminate entirely certain foods—cookies, ice cream, butter, or sometimes whole food groups—from their diets. Characterizing the needed change in such simple terms serves to make behavioral change both imaginable and manageable. It does nothing, however, to prepare one for discrepancies that tend to exist between the image of change and the realities of efforts needed to make change.

Two important points about teacher change have emerged from my study. One major idea is that changing mathematics teaching as an experienced teacher does not come about by abandoning all past practices and trying to begin again as though one had never taught before. Most current notions of learning suggest that people learn by building on prior experiences and bringing to bear what they already know as they make sense of new situations. The same is true for relearning to teach. A second major idea is that changing practice does not come about by making announcements about what one should no longer do. If a list of "don'ts" is offered, it may imply that what is needed is simply a new and better list of "dos." It is important to understand that my struggle with change was not because I was operating from a wrong or inadequate list of "things to do." The difficulty was that conceptualizing change in terms of a fixed view of teaching—dichotomies and lists of dos and don'ts—seriously underestimated the change process as well as the complex, constructive nature of the practice being learned.

Abandoning Past Practices: To Tell or Not to Tell

Telling students how to do particular math problems and whether their answers were right or wrong are examples of teacher behaviors I expected that I would need to entirely abandon. My failed efforts to completely eliminate telling forced me to reconsider the place of telling in my past teaching and the relationship between this particular teacher behavior and past and new views of mathematical knowledge, theories of learning, and images of teaching. The boundaries of telling and not telling began to blur as I moved away from seeing them as opposite elements of a teacher's practice. Just as the intonation of a statement can denote a question, so can a question be constructed in such a way as to indicate telling. Many of the questions around the use of the Minicomputer for working multiplication problems could be said to be of a "telling nature," in that they pressed for convergence. Many had a single right answer and were not at all about exploring mathematical ideas. Another example of telling is found in Sipho's observation of the discrepancies in multiple measurements of a single can in the midst of a series of lessons around making labels for cans. In this example, Sipho's observation narrows the focus but does so in a way that highlights a mathematical idea and moves the whole group forward in thinking about measurement. The telling I did in my interactions with Arif around the composition of functions in the context of multiplication and the use of the Minicomputer is another example of using telling to narrow the focus and, in doing so, illustrate something important about the mathematics. These latter two examples, with similar ones occurring in other lessons throughout the year, are what have helped me to reconsider shunning the role of telling in teaching mathematics for understanding.

I also needed to become actively engaged in deciding from moment to moment whether to tell, what to tell, to whom, and when. The series of lessons around the addition of fractions is a good example of what it means for a teacher to struggle to figure out what to tell that will make a difference. In that series of lessons, my difficulties with figuring out what to do next were connected in important ways to what it was that I understood about the mathematics and what students understood. Decisions whether to tell depend on learning how to assess students' understanding as an ongoing part of teaching in ways that illustrate whether what was told made a difference in students' understanding.

Replacing Past Practices: Changing the Textbook

While there were some teaching practices, like telling, I thought I needed to completely abandon, there were other elements of my practice I thought I needed to replace. For example, I envisioned that the assumption from my old practice that a teacher follows a prescribed curriculum as represented by a mathematics textbook would be replaced by the expectation that a teacher constructs the curriculum with her students. In a context where students were supposed to construct their own understandings of mathematical ideas as a means of learning, I expected that such a change in teaching would mean that authority for the curriculum would be transferred from the textbook to students. However, I was frightened at the thought of giving students any control over the curriculum when I felt so uncertain. At the time, a reasonable alternative was to make use of a new mathematics textbook, one in which the pedagogy and content were intended to be more like what reformers had in mind than other, more rule-based and computation-driven texts. Following a new textbook seemed like a reasonable way to begin to change my practice. It gave me a place to start by giving me rich and worthwhile tasks to use in my classroom. This line of thinking is not unlike the thoughts of many policy makers and school reformers who promote the adoption of new textbooks as a means of changing teaching. Changing practice, however, did not turn out to be as easy as changing textbooks. The textbook supported but also hindered my learning.

I had two expectations for this new teacher's guide when I started using it. One was that it could cover for the mathematics I did not understand. Another was that it would help me to respond to students. In reality, relying too heavily on the teacher's guide did not produce the teaching I imagined I was after. The need for my own understanding of the mathematics became evident through its absence. Without a deep understanding of the mathematics I wanted students to learn, I lacked the intellectual flexibility to interpret and build on a variety of students' ideas or to veer from the textbook. Clinging to the text constrained my ability to move moment by moment. Loosening my grip on the teacher's guide, left me free to be responsive to students. I became in control of what to do next.

I was learning how to take an active role in constructing the curriculum with students. The making of labels for cans is an example of this. What was intended as a one-day lesson by the teacher's guide evolved into a series of lessons based on students' interests in the problem. The lesson about multiplication in the context of the composition of functions is an example of how I was learning to take control of the curriculum in the moment-to-moment work of teaching as I continually figured out how to interpret and build on students' ideas. Following the mathematics textbook two pages at a time, problem by problem, as I had done for many years as a teacher, and before that as a student, was no longer an appropriate thing to do. I was learning to put myself in a different relationship to the curriculum. The curriculum was not something disconnected from me, my interpretation of the immediate situation, my understandings of the mathematics, or students' understandings.

I needed to learn to see myself as capable of constructing knowledge about content and pedagogy. I needed, however, to do more than just believe I was capable. I had to learn to think and reason about what made mathematical and pedagogical sense to do next. Making the change from following a prescribed curriculum to one in which the students' ideas and mine played a major role in curriculum construction was not a simple matter of transferring authority from the textbook to students. I needed to regard myself as a key player who mediated the use of a text as well as students' ideas.

Moving Away from Dichotomies

The realities of practice changed my conception of what was entailed in teaching mathematics for understanding and revised my expectations for what it might take to make changes in my practice. Framing the contrasts between old and new practice in terms of dichotomies of skills was not useful. Abandoning or replacing elements of teaching was a far too simple way to view teacher change. When I realized the inadequacy of the dichotomies, I found myself having to invent a practice. Sometimes the work was as specific as figuring out what to say or do next. Other times, the work entailed more general thinking about purposes and possible next moves.

I have a new appreciation for a chart I borrowed from the *Curriculum and Evaluation Standards for School Mathematics* (NCTM, 1989) and presented in the Introduction (see Figure I.1). Without looking carefully, one could easily construe the left- and right-hand columns to be representative of new and old practices. In short, this chart could be seen as a list of shoulds and should nots. I now appreciate the headings "increased attention", "decreased attention", and how they relate to each of the columns. They are new and old ideas about teaching mathematics that teachers learn to compose in a variety of ways to varying degrees at different points during teaching.

THE NEED FOR SUBJECT MATTER KNOWLEDGE

The need for teachers to have more subject matter knowledge is a common refrain in teacher education. Few researchers, however, have confronted head on what mathematics it is that teachers need to know. Doing the analyses of teaching was an opportunity for me to explore, in depth, the mathematics it might have been useful to have known at the time I taught those lessons. I recognize that this is an opportunity most elementary teachers would not have time to pursue. Looking back on the chapters of this book, I contemplate what I learned about the nature of the mathematics that I needed to learn. Shulman (1986) identifies theoretically the intersection between subject matter knowledge and teaching as "pedagogical content knowledge." He claims that it is one of several components of the broader construct of strategic knowledge (Shulman, 1986)—a theoretical construct for the knowledge needed to make moment-to-moment decisions in situations where principles of practice are not helpful. Many of the previous studies on subject matter knowledge in teaching looked at novices' development of these kinds of teacher knowledge, novices who had had opportunities to learn the subject matter followed by opportunities to learn how to use their subject matter knowledge in teaching. My study tackles issues related to the simultaneous acquisition and use of mathematical knowledge in the course of teaching.

Not Enough Knowledge

I began this teaching expecting that what I would have to learn was more mathematics than what I knew. I imagined that as I taught, I would discover what I needed to learn. I expected the day to come, admittedly, perhaps not during that year, when I could say that I understood the mathematics I needed to know, and the teaching of mathematics for understanding would, henceforth, become easier.

As I made my way through the lessons in the mathematics textbook, mathematical questions arose for me. For example, I started being concerned that I did not understand the relevance of patterns as they related to functions. The connection and importance were implied within the text but they were not anything I could understand at the time. The mathematical questions that arose for me across these lessons could not necessarily be answered by learning *more* math. Rather, the mathematics I needed to learn involved taking a new look at the mathematics I thought I understood. Clearly, the difficulties of the changes I tried to make in my teaching were not because I did not know *enough* mathematics. Rather, the difficulties arose because it seemed that the mathematics I needed to understand was qualitatively different from the mathematics I thought I understood.

A Different Kind of Knowledge

When my expectations shifted from the need to know more mathematics to the need to know a qualitatively different kind of mathematics, my expectation of ever knowing or mastering all the mathematics I needed to know vanished. Rather, the nature of what I was learning I needed to understand was at a level of ideas fundamental to the study of mathematics. I was learning to look for and ask fundamental questions—questions without clear right or wrong answers over which people throughout history with varying degrees of mathematical interest and expertise have struggled, argued, and debated.

An example of the complexity of the mathematical ideas to which I am referring can be found surrounding the issues that arose in the context of the problem I gave students that dealt with addition of two fractions with like denominators: $3/4 + 2/4$. I went into this lesson knowing the answer was $5/4$, based on my past experiences with learning and teaching the rule needed to solve this problem: When adding fractions with like denominators, add only the numerators and keep the denominators the same. I also anticipated a common error of adding the denominators. Therefore, $5/8$ might be a common but wrong answer. I thought learning this math problem "for understanding" would mean being able to come up with a reason why it made sense to not add the denominators. I worked from the assumption that there was a single right answer and it was my responsibility in the context of this kind of mathematics teaching to help students come up with reasons to explain why that was the case.

Much to my surprise, the answer that I thought was undeniably wrong—$5/8$—was, under certain conditions, a reasonable answer (see Chapter 7). Under further investigation, I learned that what students and I were trying to understand—issues about the unit—was a major theme in the history of the development of rational numbers. In the process of working on this problem with students, I had hit upon a key to understanding fractions—what is the whole? I expanded my expectations and sparked my own curiosities about what it could mean to understand the addition of fractions "for understanding."

New Expectations for Knowing Subject Matter

One of the major things I learned about subject matter knowledge is that acquiring and using it are going to be ongoing intellectual challenges in teaching. Ongoing learning of mathematics is intimately connected to this kind of teaching. I give three reasons to support this claim. First, I learned that there is a mathematical territory defined by fundamental questions and ideas to be constructed and reconstructed through investigations by teachers and students that is qualitatively different from anything I learned in the past. Second, the problems, activities, and representations I used with students were tools for learning the mathematical ideas that were important. They were not important in and of themselves. Therefore, part of the intellectual work of teaching becomes trying to see the fundamental mathematical ideas in textbook problems, activities, and representations where the connections to larger mathematical ideas are not necessarily made explicit. A third piece of intellectual work is learning to hear these fundamental ideas in students' efforts to communicate mathematical ideas they may be on the edge of understanding. It takes a keen ear and a flexible mind to interpret and build connections from students' vague notions of mathematical sense to a vast territory of mathematical knowledge that is dynamic and fluid in nature.

In retrospect, I can see that I pushed my understanding of the mathematical ideas in each lesson to a place where I bumped up against a fundamental mathematical question or idea. I confronted the fundamental mathematical ideas underlying patterns and functions, multiplication, and fractions, in the analyses of three different teaching events. In the analysis of a fourth series of lessons, I confronted an issue central to doing mathematics within a mathematical community—the intermingling of the social and intellectual, and the tensions and issues that arise as the two interact as a means of learning mathematics. This view of mathematical knowledge (Davis & Hersh, 1981; Kitcher, 1984; Lakatos, 1976)—both what is to be known and how one comes to know—revised my expectation that one ever could completely know mathematics.

Teaching for understanding necessitates that the influence on what one knows mathematically travel in multiple directions—from teachers to students, students to teachers, and students to students. All participants need to expect to learn from one another. Teachers still need to prepare for the situation by learning prior to the situation what they can about the mathematics they are about to teach. Questions still remain about where and how teachers are going to get help learning what they need to know. Prepared with some sense of the territory in which they might explore with students, teachers could enter the classroom curious about the sense students make of ideas, expecting that what they learn about their students' understandings may reshape how they see things, raise new questions about what it is that they think they understand, reshape the purposes of whatever it is they thought they were doing, and change anything that they may have had in mind to do.

TEACHING AS LEARNING

What I did not expect, but soon came to learn, was that making changes in teaching involved more than dealing with the intellectual challenges of my own knowing and not knowing of subject matter. I was unprepared for the questions that arose for me and others about who I thought I was and what I thought I knew about teaching.

The Risks of Being a Learner

It felt like an enormous risk—to be headed into a fourth-grade mathematics class when I knew I had much to learn about what I was supposed to be teaching. The risk felt magnified by the fact that I would not be trying to make these changes alone, with students, behind the closed door of my classroom. Instead, there would be people watching—the teacher who taught these students all of the other subjects, a researcher, and a teacher educator. At first it felt threatening. Would I be able to take such risks in front of other people, people who represented broader categories of people who traditionally are considered knowers about teaching—experienced teachers, researchers, teacher educators? What would they think of me? What would they say about me to others? The only time I had had people watch me teach in the past, the purpose had been evaluation.

The people who had planned to observe me teach that year had all promised that evaluation was not their purpose. Could I trust them? Would they appreciate the problems I faced? The classroom teacher had twice my number of years of teaching experience. Would she view me as a rookie whose problems could easily be solved by experience? Reineke, the researcher, had been interested in studying the students' and my changing conceptions of mathematics. At the time, I did not understand his question—math was math, wasn't it? Would he view me as a less than qualified practitioner because I was unfamiliar with the theories that undergirded his work as a researcher? Lampert, the teacher educator, had offered to help me teach differently, to think through the pedagogical and mathematical problems I would face as I tried to make changes. She had assured me she would not be there to judge me. Could I believe her? She was a university professor. I was her student. Evaluation was always wrapped up in teacher–student relationships, wasn't it?

Much to my surprise, I learned that I could trust each of these people. For example, the classroom teacher supported my efforts one hundred percent in front of those to whom my performance might have mattered—the students, the students' parents, other teachers, and the school's administrator. In our private conversations, she sometimes questioned what I did. She wondered aloud about why I might have made one choice over another. But in the presence of others, she voiced admiration for the changes I tried to make, sympathized with my struggles, and wanted others to understand what she and I were learning from my efforts. At any given moment, I felt as if we shared the responsibility for what students were learning. Reineke, the researcher, quickly abandoned his initial agenda of keeping a distanced position as he "researched" my changing conceptions of mathematics. My interviews with him became conversations in which we pondered together questions of mathematical content and pedagogy. He entered graduate school when I did and was no further along in understanding this kind of mathematics teaching than I was. Lampert was at once a wise teacher in the role of a teacher educator and an empathetic colleague who taught mathematics in the fifth-grade classroom next door to me. I found that she took my questions seriously and respected my past teaching experiences as well as all of my efforts to try something new. Oddly enough, she seemed excited when I recognized things I did not know, when she and I could discuss questions I was able to articulate.

In a strange way, over time within these relationships with people who I expected would intimidate me, I found myself protected and sheltered, appreciated and celebrated for being a learner. Each grew sympathetic to my struggles and, together, we developed shared understandings of what was happening. Teaching only mathematics, 4 days a week, gave me the time to focus on mathematics teaching that most elementary teachers never have. My schedule allowed me to take advantage of 5-minute unplanned conversations with the classroom teacher before and after my teaching. It allowed me to schedule biweekly conversations with Reineke in conjunction with his observations. It enabled me to observe in Lampert's fifth-grade mathematics class at least as often as she observed in mine and to talk with her several times a week. Together, these relationships provided a rich context for sustained conversations about mathematics, students, and pedagogy with people who, for a variety of reasons, were closely connected to my practice.

The Risks of Claiming to Be a Learner and a Teacher

I felt so accepted as a learner by these three different people that year, that I was painfully surprised the first few times I tried to talk about my learning with a wider circle of teachers, researchers, and teacher educators less familiar with me and my experiences. I found that many of these participants in the larger culture of teaching did not have the same appreciation for the problems of practice I had come to share with the classroom teacher, Reineke, and Lampert.

For example, on several different occasions, shortly after I finished that year of teaching, I told the story of what happened as students tried to reason about the addition of $\frac{3}{4}$ and $\frac{2}{4}$. I was intrigued by the complex mathematical and pedagogical issues raised by students' diverse understandings of the problem. I tried to initiate a conversation about these issues. Much to my surprise, no one wanted to discuss them. One by one, those who had listened to me unveil my problems offered me suggestions for what I should have done differently. My problems were viewed as simple, and the solutions as obvious.

My fellow educators wanted to be supportive, but we viewed my teaching differently. On the one hand, they saw $\frac{5}{4}$ as right and felt it was their responsibility to give me ways to get students to see that. On the other hand, I was beginning to see the "sense" in $\frac{5}{8}$ and wanted to talk about why. What I was concerned about could not be fixed by suggesting that I try this or do that. No one but me seemed to see the teaching, or the mathematics I was trying to help students learn, as inherently difficult. At the time, I could not understand what was happening. I fought back feelings of inadequacy and frustration. Part of me felt bad for not knowing, thinking that I should have known, while another part of me had spent a year learning to appreciate the value of not knowing, of never being certain, in a practice that was improvised. Why couldn't these people see the complexity I could? I feared I appeared to others as incompetent for having questions about practice, the same questions that I had been praised for recognizing and that others had pondered with me during the year I taught. Consequently, on those several occasions, I walked away fighting back tears as I questioned who I was, what I knew, and what it was I was supposed to know. I worried that people had just explained away the difficulties I had making changes in my practice, thinking that the real problem was that I was an incompetent teacher. I imagined questions people must have been asking themselves. How could she be such a bad teacher and be allowed to become a teacher educator with a Ph.D.?

Painful as these experiences were, they helped me to see two additional things necessary to make change. One is to begin to rephrase the questions we ask about teaching, to move from pedagogical questions that have single right answers and imply a perfect method, technique, or strategy, to questions that imply a complex practice filled with intellectual, pedagogical, and moral dilemmas (Lampert, 1986). Second, those who teach, teach others to teach, do research on those who teach, or evaluate those who teach need to learn to talk and act in ways that acknowledge teaching as inherently complex and uncertain. The challenge is to reconstruct a culture of teaching whereby it becomes intellectually possible and emotionally feasible for teachers, administrators, researchers, and teacher educators, traditional authorities on teaching, to appreciate the inherent complexities of teaching mathematics for understanding and to view themselves and be viewed by others as certified learners rather than knowers of teaching—lifelong constructors of knowledge of an uncertain practice.

EDUCATING TEACHERS FOR UNCERTAINTY

This is not to say that all must be learned by trial and error. Contemplating how to teach teachers to teach mathematics for understanding entails thinking about how to prepare teachers to perform an uncertain activity.[1] Not only has teaching been redefined through the reforms in mathematics education, but ways of helping teachers also must be revisioned to include the uncertain, spontaneous nature of teaching. Yinger's (1988) notion of preparation is helpful in its contrast of the more conventional notion of "planning" with that of "preparation."

> Planning seeks to deal with uncertainty by controlling action and outcomes. The goal is to constrain the unpredictable, the random, and the wild. On the other hand, preparation acknowledges our limited ability to predict and the constructive nature of life. Preparation expects diversity, surprise, the random, and the wild. To prepare is to get ready, to become equipped, and to become receptive. The focus of preparation is on oneself, not on a framework to constrain possibility. In a sense, preparation enlarges the future. (p. 88)

Preparation for teaching mathematics for understanding is about learning what to expect from and during practice and being prepared to act on whatever happens, even the unexpected.

Educative Curricula: The Textbook

I was thrilled at the onset of my teaching to have the CSMP curriculum at my disposal. It represented mathematics in ways that looked different from what I had learned as a student, and the pedagogy was designed around a set of problems intended for students to solve that did not look anything like the computation I had had students doing for years. I expected that the teacher's guide would take care of the mathematics I did not understand and the scripted dialogue would serve as a guide for how to respond to students. At the time, given the content and design of CSMP, these seemed like reasonable expectations.

However, while the mathematics within CSMP was, indeed, represented in conceptual ways, it was not in a form that was accessible to me. It was insufficient for the understanding of the mathematics to be contained within the textbook and not within *me*. While teaching, I quickly saw the need to possess an understanding of the mathematics myself. I saw the same need with respect to understanding students. While having possible student responses represented in a scripted dialogue within the teacher's guide gave me some idea of what to expect from students, students' ideas often were formulated differently from the responses predicted in the teacher's guide. I quickly found myself at a pedagogical disadvantage as I tried to hear those responses in the language of students. Without an understanding of the mathematics or the relevance of particular responses, I could not discern the mathematical significance within responses and floundered as I contemplated what to do next. These two responsibilities—understanding the content and responding to students—which I initially saw as residing with the textbook, I now see as inherently the teacher's. Rather than dismiss the notion of a mathematics textbook entirely, however, it is sensible to rethink how a textbook might help teachers meet these responsibilities. This is at least a two-part agenda. One aspect involves rethinking *how to make use of the textbook*. A second part of the change involves rethinking the *contents of the textbook*.

Attention to Mathematical Content. What is needed is a curriculum for teachers that is based on the premise that mathematical knowledge is socially constructed, while at the same time recognizing that there are particular problems, questions, and ideas that are important to grapple with. It would be helpful to know what is conventional agreed-upon mathematical knowledge and which ideas are open to interpretation. Teachers need help understanding the connections between the problems and activities intended for students and the important mathematical ideas the problems and activities are intended to teach. Problems and activities are used as means, not ends, for understanding.

Given that there is such a strong need in this kind of mathematics teaching to be responsive to students' ideas, it is helpful for curriculum materials to provide likely student responses, as CSMP has done. But in addition, teachers need help interpreting what they hear their own students say. Verbatim quotes of likely student responses are not very useful without some understanding of *why* these might be typical responses. What mathematics would someone understand who would say these things? What might someone say who did not have a good understanding of the mathematics? What might be reasonable alternative responses? This kind of additional information in a text would provide a context for teachers to assess and make use of their students' responses relative to the mathematics they are trying to teach—an integral part of what is demanded in teaching mathematics for understanding.

In short, teachers need access to the mathematical knowledge of ideas and connections and relationships in textbooks that is possessed by curriculum developers, who now take responsibility for constructing pedagogical paths through the mathematical terrain that teachers follow. Curricular materials are needed that make visible how pathways through the mathematical terrain are constructed by such things as choices of problems to give students and teachers' next moves. Teachers need to understand the grounds on which decisions are made about possible problems or activities to do with students. They also need to learn what goes into decisions about what to do next so that they can learn to make their own decisions and construct their own paths, ones that are responsive to their particular students. The teacher's guides to most current mathematics textbooks provide a single path through the terrain of mathematics, with few of the curricular decisions of the developers made visible to users.

Attention to Teachers' Learning. In earlier reforms of mathematics education, curriculum developers went to great lengths to design "teacher proof" materials, curriculum materials intended to keep teachers distanced from teaching, learning, and content (Sarason, 1982). The nature of teaching mathematics for understanding demands that the teacher be intimately connected to the decisions that govern the teaching and learning of content. Curriculum developers must find ways to guide teachers' pedagogical and mathematical decisions rather than make decontextualized decisions for them. One primary way to help teachers to do this is by finding ways to increase teachers' understandings of the content. For example, in the case of rational numbers, curriculum materials could offer a teacher help in thinking through the mathematical issues related to the addition of fractions. Teachers could be alerted to the difficulties students might encounter in identifying and keeping the unit constant, by providing explanations of the reasonableness behind such difficulties. Teachers also could be helped to understand the usefulness of particular contexts or representations for understanding particular ideas.

To think of teachers as learners when designing curriculum is something that occurred to Bruner (1960/1977) many years ago, in the context of earlier reforms in education, but few textbook developers have heeded this thinking. Bruner (1960/1977), in a preface to a new edition of *The Process of Education*, wrote:

> A curriculum is more for teachers than it is for pupils. If it cannot change, move, perturb, inform teachers, it will have no effect on those whom they teach. It must be first and foremost a curriculum for teachers. If it has any effect on pupils, it will have it by virtue of having had an effect on teachers. (p. xv)

Perhaps one of the reasons why Bruner's (1960/1977) advice has not been followed is that few curriculum developers have understood why it was important or what it might mean to attend to teachers' learning, and few educators have taken seriously the need for elementary teachers to understand subject matter—in this case, mathematics. If one thinks teaching is about particular behaviors, then telling through textbooks is a sufficient and efficient way to help teachers. Curriculum materials have been directing teachers about what to do for years. As Cohen and Barnes (1993) note, teachers need opportunities to learn from new curricula that are similar to the learning that reformers intend for students. We need curriculum materials that are educative rather than directive.

Educating Teachers: Acquiring the Tools of Invention

My study implies that the emphasis of helping teachers change their practice should shift away from helping teachers learn new skills or strategies and away from supplying them with new math problems and manipulatives—specifics of what or how to teach—toward learning how to create and recognize choices and make decisions about appropriate math problems, representations, and responses to further students' understandings.

I purposefully make no distinctions here between the education of preservice and practicing teachers. There are two reasons for this. The first is a substantive reason. While I remain uncertain about the exact differences that years of teaching experience might make as one attempts to teach in ways aligned with the reforms, I believe that what I have learned would apply equally to preservice teachers. The nature of the teaching that one is continuously aiming to invent is the same for both a novice and a veteran teacher. Preservice teachers, admittedly, will need additional understandings to compensate for what they might lack without the benefit of past teaching experiences; however, just what they might need is beyond the scope of this study. The second reason I do not distinguish here between preservice and inservice teacher education relates to the question of *how* teachers are going to learn what they need to, which, admittedly, could vary considerably whether one is referring to preservice or inservice teachers.

Learning the Mathematical Territory and How to Explore It. It would be impossible within the confines of any single teacher education experience, whether a preservice methods course or a one-shot inservice workshop, to help teachers construct a qualitatively different kind of understanding of mathematics in all topics of the elementary curriculum. Therefore, one is faced with issues of breadth versus depth in contemplating whether to explore a multitude of mathematical topics in limited depth or a few topics in greater depth. Given the past mathematical learning experiences of most teachers and the nature of the teaching they are aiming to do, I argue that it is important for teachers to have the experience of learning a few areas of mathematics in depth and to apply what was learned from that experience to learning something new. To learn how to teach an area of mathematics in depth means acquiring particular understandings of the topic as well as gaining a perspective on what it means to learn and construct new mathematical ideas.

For example, what would it mean to take what one understands about fractions from a study of the topic and apply that experience to efforts to learn another area of mathematics, like probability? How does learning one topic in depth prepare one to learn another? In my case, I learned ways to begin an exploration of an area of mathematics for which I have little understanding. I learned that one way to begin is by seeing what others have learned who have already spent time exploring the territory from other perspectives, for other purposes. This could mean finding people to talk with: mathematicians who understand the subject matter or teachers who have taught the topic in depth.

It also could mean reading research in mathematics education done mainly by cognitive psychologists, who do research on how students understand particular mathematical ideas, or what has been written about probability in the history of mathematics. What one is after in pursuing these sources are some tentative understandings of the difficulties, problems, and main challenges people have confronted in their efforts to make sense of a particular area of mathematics. To have an understanding of a mathematical topic means having a sense, at some fundamental level, of what one understands, what it means to understand, and what one has left to learn.

I have gained a sense for how to use resources and I also have learned how to ask questions of myself and others to get at the important mathematical ideas found in math problems, representations, and students' responses. Simple questions, like what is a pattern or what does it mean to multiply, have complex solutions, grounded in assumptions and conditions that, when one tries to understand them, place one at the center of what it means to understand mathematical ideas in a deep and fundamental way.

Learning to Appreciate Children as Knowers. I have learned to be concerned about students' understanding in relation to my own. I have learned the need for trusting the reasonableness of all students' intuitions, especially those whom, for a variety of reasons, I may least expect to have helpful interpretations of mathematical ideas.

My interactions with Jennifer regarding patterns (see Chapter 1), have helped me see that what a teacher can hear in what students say may be as indicative of what a teacher understands about the mathematics as about what students understand. That is, what teachers are able to interpret from what students say is highly dependent on what teachers themselves understand about the mathematics. When a teacher has difficulty interpreting what a particular student is trying to communicate, the norm is for the teacher to question the student's understanding. An equally important thing to do is for teachers to question their own mathematical understandings. It is not the students' responsibility to match their understandings with the teacher's. It is the teacher's responsibility to push him- or herself to make sense of what it is that students understand. The series of lessons around $3/4 + 2/4$ (see Chapter 7) is a good example of making an effort to try to understand the assumptions and conditions under which the "obviously wrong answer," $5/8$, *could* make sense. For this to happen, it means that a teacher needs to learn to work from the premise that what students say makes sense, and to learn to understand how. My interactions with Sipho (see Chapter 5) help to illustrate the potential of all students, even those one may least expect, to make meaningful contributions to their own learning and the learning of others. Expecting to be surprised by what students understand rather than disappointed by what they do not understand is a useful stance to learn to take toward students.

Learning to Construct and Reconstruct Pedagogy. Understanding pedagogy means having a sense of pedagogical problems or dilemmas to expect in the context of teaching and, over time, accruing insight and experience that enable one to construct and reconstruct tentative solutions. I offer two examples of things that I have learned about pedagogy that have helped me learn what to expect. It is not that I have mastered leading a discussion or that I have learned how to construct the perfect curriculum. Rather, I have learned things I need to be aware of, questions I need to ask as I try to lead a discussion and reconsider what it means to cover the curriculum.

Through my efforts to hold a discussion, I have learned some important ideas about what discussions demand of teachers. For example, a teacher needs an understanding of the mathematics she is trying to teach so that she has some sense of what there is to discuss. This knowledge of what there is to talk about comes from a study of the mathematical territory, as described in an earlier section, where one begins to learn what fundamental questions and ideas are worth spending time talking about. Related to this, one needs an ongoing sense of purpose. What is it that is important for students to learn? Had I understood this, I might have done a better job sustaining a worthwhile discussion of patterns.

I also have learned to think differently about pedagogy in the context of curriculum. I have learned to reconsider the question of what it means to "cover the curriculum." I have learned to think about curriculum more as layers of concepts or a web of relationships with single problems cutting through layers or sitting in the center of a web of ideas than as a scope and sequence of behavioral objectives. If I had thought about curriculum like this, I would have started out with a different purpose for doing the problem $3/4 + 2/4$. I would have seen the muffin problem as a rich context for students to explore the issue of representing the unit rather than as merely an occasion to reason about the rule of not adding the denominators.

Learning to Trust Oneself. Learning to continuously invent a practice means learning to regard oneself as the inventor of a practice. What it takes to be an inventor of practice encompasses learning about all of these things—mathematics, students, and pedagogy—simultaneously, none of which can be known by its being told to someone. This means facing oneself as a thinker, someone capable of figuring out what makes sense. It entails considering what one knows and trusting oneself to make decisions based on what one knows, however tentative. It means learning that it is one's role to think for oneself as a teacher. If one comes to see oneself in this light, expectations for what it means to be educated as a teacher are altered.

For example, had I entered this year of teaching seeing myself as the inventor of a practice, I would have expected mathematical questions to arise for which I did not have an answer. A question like, "What is a pattern?" would have been viewed as the source of a lively discussion rather than as a simple question for which there was an identifiable right answer that I just did not know. I would have expected to wonder about students' intuitions when solving problems. I would have capitalized on the mathematical sense behind students' use of a ruler to try to add fractions rather than brushing off their efforts as confusing nonsense or a venture off the track. And, finally, I would have appreciated that continuously asking the question of what to do next is what propels teaching. It does not represent a shortcoming or a question for which there will ever be a single right answer. It represents a view of knowledge about teaching, children, and mathematics that is tentative and uncertain, constructed and reconstructed in the act of teaching.

NOTES

1. I borrow this idea of preparing for uncertainty from an article by Floden and Clark (1988) in which they discuss, in general terms, preparing teachers for uncertainty.

References

Arcavi, A., Bruckheimer, M., & Bens-zvi, R. (1987). History of mathematics for teachers: The case of irrational numbers. *For the Learning of Mathematics*, *7*(2), 18–23.

Ashton-Warner, S. (1963). *Teacher*. New York: Simon & Schuster.

Atweh, B., Bleicher, R. E., & Cooper, T. J. (1998). The construction of the social context of mathematics classrooms: A sociolinguistic analysis. *Journal for Research in Mathematics Education*, *29*(1), 63–82.

Ball, D. L. (1990). Reflections and deflections of policy: The case of Carol Turner. *Educational Evaluation and Policy Analysis*, *12*(3), 237–249.

Ball, D. L. (1993a). Halves, pieces, and twoths: Constructing representational contexts in teaching fractions. In T. Carpenter, E. Fennema, & T. Romberg (Eds.), *Rational numbers: An integration of research* (pp. 157–196). Hillsdale, NJ: Erlbaum.

Ball, D. L. (1993b). With an eye on the mathematical horizon: Dilemmas of teaching elementary school mathematics. *Elementary School Journal*, *93*(4), 373–397.

Ball, D. L., & Rundquist, S. S. (1993). Collaboration as a context for joining teacher learning with learning about teaching. In D. K. Cohen, M. W. McLaughlin, & J. E. Talbert (Eds.), *Teaching for understanding: Challenges for policy and practice* (pp. 13–42). San Francisco: Jossey-Bass.

Becker, J. P., & Selter, C. (1996). Elementary school practices. In A. J. Bishop et al. (Eds.), *International handbook of mathematics education* (pp. 511–564). Netherlands: Kluwer Academic.

Behr, M. J., Harel, G., Post, T., & Lesh, R. (1994). Units of quantity: A conceptual basis common to additive and multiplicative structures. In G. Harel & J. Confrey (Eds.), *The development of multiplicative reasoning in the learning of mathematics* (pp. 121–176). Albany: State Uuniversity of New York Press.

Behr, M. J., Lesh, R., Post, T. R., & Silver, E. A. (1983). Rational-number concepts. In R. Lesh & M. Landau (Eds.), *Acquisition of mathematics concepts and processes* (pp. 91–126). New York: Academic Press.

Behr, M. J., & Post, T. R. (1988). Teaching rational number and decimal concepts. In T. R. Post (Ed.), *Teaching mathematics in grades K–8* (pp. 190–231). Boston: Allyn & Bacon.

Blom, L. A., & Chaplin, L. T. (1988). *The moment of movement*. Pittsburgh: University of Pittsburgh Press.

Bruner, J. (1977). *The process of education*. Cambridge, MA: Harvard University Press. (Original work published 1960)

Burnaford, G., Fischer, J., & Hobson, D. (1996). *Teachers doing research: Practical possibilities*. Mahwah, NJ: Erlbaum.

California State Department of Education. (1985). *Mathematics framework for California public schools, kindergarten through grade twelve*. Sacramento: Author.

California State Department of Education. (1992). *Mathematics framework for California public schools, kindergarten through grade twelve*. Sacramento: Author.

Calkins, L. M. (1983). *Lessons from a child: On the teaching and learning of writing*. Melbourne: Heinemann.

Carpenter, T. P., & Fennema, E. (1988). Research and cognitively guided instruction. In E. Fennema, T. P. Carpenter, & S. J. Lamon (Eds.), *Integrating research on teaching and learning mathematics* (pp. 2–19). Madison: University of Wisconsin, Wisconsin Center for Education Research.

Carter, K. (1993). The place of story in the study of teaching and teacher education. *Educational Researcher*, *22*(1), 5–12.

Cazden, C. (1992). *Whole language plus: Essays on literacy in the U.S. and New Zealand*. New York: Teachers College Press.

CEMREL. (1981). *The CSMP approach to curriculum development*. St. Louis: Author.

CEMREL. (1982). *Comprehensive school mathematics program*. Report to the joint dissemination review panel. St. Louis: Author.

Clarke, D. M. (1997). The changing role of the mathematics teacher. *Journal for Research in Mathematics Education*, *28*(3), 278–306.

Cobb, P., Wood, T., Yackel, E., & McNeal, B. (1992). Characteristics of classroom mathematics traditions: An interactional analysis. *American Educational Research Journal*, *29*(3), 573–604.

Cochran-Smith, M., & Lytle, S. L. (1993). *Inside/Outside: Teacher research and knowledge*. New York: Teachers College Press.

Cohen, D. K. (1988). Teaching practice: Plus ça change. In P. W. Jackson (Ed.), *Contributing to educational change: Perspectives on research and practice* (pp. 27–84). Berkeley: McCutchan.

Cohen, D. K. (1990). A revolution in one classroom: The case of Mrs. Oublier. *Educational Evaluation and Policy Analysis*, *12*(3), 311–329.

Cohen, D. K., & Ball, D. L. (1990). Relations between policy and practice: A commentary. *Educational Evaluation and Policy Analysis*, *12*(3), 331–338.

Cohen, D. K., & Barnes, C. A. (1993). Pedagogy and policy. In D. Cohen, M. McLaughlin, & J. Talbert (Eds.), *Teaching for understanding: Challenges for policy and practice* (pp. 240–275). San Francisco: Jossey-Bass.

Cohen, D. K., & Hill, H. (1997). *Instructional policy and classroom performance: The mathematics reform in California. CPRE Research Report*. Philadelphia: University of Pennsylvania, CPRE.

Cohen, D. K., McLaughlin, M. W., & Talbert, J. E. (Eds.). (1993). *Teaching for understanding: Challenges for policy and practice.* San Francisco: Jossey-Bass.

Cuban, L. (1990). What I learned from what I had forgotten about teaching: Notes from a professor. *Phi Delta Kappan, 71*(6), 479–482.

Darling-Hammond, L. (1994). Developing professional development schools: Early lessons, challenge, and promise. In L. Darling-Hammond (Ed.), *Professional development schools* (pp. 1–27). New York: Teachers College Press.

Darling-Hammond, L. (1997). *Doing what matters most: Investing in quality teaching.* New York: National Commission on Teaching and America's Future.

Davis, B. (1996). *Teaching mathematics: Toward a sound alternative.* New York: Garland.

Davis, B. (1997). Listening for differences: An evolving conception of mathematics teaching. *Journal for Research in Mathematics Education, 28*(3), 355–376.

Davis, P. J., & Hersch, R. (1981). *The mathematical experience.* Boston: Birkhauser.

Dean, R. T. (1989). *Creative improvisation.* Stratford, UK: Open University Press.

Dennison, G. (1969). *The lives of children: The story of the First Street School.* New York: Vantage Books.

Dewey, J. (1966). *Democracy and education.* New York: Free Press. (Original work published 1916)

Dow, P. B. (1991). *Schoolhouse politics.* Cambridge, MA: Harvard University Press.

Eggleston, E. (1899). *The Hoosier schoolmaster.* New York: Grosset & Dunlap.

Eicholz, R. E., O'Daffer, P. G., Feelnor, C. R., Charles, R. I., Young, S., & Barnett, C. (1987). *Addison-Wesley mathematics.* Menlo Park, CA: Addison-Wesley.

Eisner, E. W. (1992). What a professor learned in the third grade. In F. K. Oser, A. Dick, & J. L. Patry (Eds.), *Effective and responsible teaching* (pp. 261–277). San Francisco: Jossey-Bass.

Eisner, E. W. (1993). Forms of understanding and the future of educational research. *Educational Researcher,* 22(7), 5–11.

Elmore, R. F., Peterson, P. L., & McCarthey, S. J. (1996). *Restructuring in the classroom: Teaching, learning, and school reorganization.* San Francisco: Jossey-Bass.

Eves, H. (1969). *An introduction to the history of mathematics.* New York: Holt, Reinhardt, and Winston.

Fawcett, H. P. (1938). *The nature of proof.* New York: Bureau of Publications, Teachers College.

Feiman-Nemser, S., & Floden, R. E. (1986). The cultures of teaching. In M. C.

Wittrock (Ed.), *Handbook of research on teaching* (pp. 505–526). New York: Macmillan.

Fennema, E., & Nelson, B. S. (1997). *Mathematics teachers in transition*. Hillsdale, NJ: Erlbaum.

Fleischer, C. (1995). *Composing teacher research: A prosaic history*. Albany: State University of New York Press.

Floden, R. E., & Clark, C. M. (1988). Preparing teachers for uncertainty. *Teachers College Record, 89*(4), 505–524.

Fuson, K. (1988). Summary comments: Meaning in middle grade number concepts. In J. Hiebert & M. Behr (Eds.), National Council of Teachers of Mathematics, *Number concepts and operations in the middle grades* (pp. 260–264). Hillsdale, NJ: Erlbaum.

Hammersley, M., & Atkinson, P. (1989). *Ethnography principles and practice*. New York: Routledge.

Harel, G., & Confrey, J. (Eds.). (1994). *The development of multiplicative reasoning in the learning of mathematics*. Albany: State University of New York Press.

Hawkins, D. (1974). I, thou, and it. In D. Hawkins, *The informed vision: Essays on learning and human nature* (pp. 48–62). New York: Agathon Press.

Heaton, R. M. (1991, February). *Continuity and connectedness in teaching and research: A self study of learning to teach mathematics for understanding*. Paper presented at the University of Pennsylvania Ethnography in Education Research Forum, Philadelphia.

Heaton, R. M. (1992). Who is minding the mathematics content? A case study of a fifth-grade teacher. *Elementary School Journal, 93*, 153–162.

Heaton, R. M., & Lampert M. (1993). Learning to hear voices: Inventing a new pedagogy of teacher education. In D. Cohen, M. McLaughlin, & J. Talbert (Eds.), *Teaching for understanding: Challenges for policy and practice* (pp. 43–83). San Francisco: Jossey-Bass.

Heaton, R. M., Reineke, J. W., & Frese, J. D. (1991, April). *Collective reflection: An account of collaborative research*. Paper presented at the annual meeting of the American Educational Research Association, Chicago.

Hiebert, J., & Behr, M. (1988). Introduction: Capturing the major themes. In J. Hiebert & M. Behr (Eds.), National Council of Teachers of Mathematics, *Number concepts and operations in the middle grades* (pp. 1–18). Hillsdale, NJ: Erlbaum.

Hiebert, J., & Lefevre, P. (1986). Conceptual and procedural knowledge in mathematics: An introductory analysis. In J. Hiebert (Ed.), *Conceptual and procedural knowledge: The case of mathematics* (pp. 1–27). Hillsdale, NJ: Erlbaum.

Hiebert, J., & Wearne, D. (1988). Methodologies for studying learning to inform teaching. In E. Fennema, T. P. Carpenter, & S. J. Lamon (Eds.), *Integrating research on teaching and learning mathematics* (pp. 168–192).

Madison: University of Wisconsin, Wisconsin Center for Education Research.

Hiebert, J., & Wearne, D. (1992). Links between teaching and learning place value with understanding in first grade. *Journal for Research in Mathematics Education, 23*(2), 98–122.

Hoffman, M. (1996). *Chasing hellhounds.* Minneapolis: Milkweed.

Hollingsworth, S., & Sockett, H. (Eds.). (1994). *Teacher research and educational reform.* Ninety-third yearbook of the National Society for the Study of Education. Chicago: University of Chicago Press.

Jackson, P. (1986). *The practice of teaching.* New York: Teachers College Press.

Karush, W. (1989). *Webster's new world dictionary of mathematics.* New York: Prentice Hall.

Kitcher, P. (1984). *The nature of mathematical knowledge.* New York: Oxford University Press.

Kline, M. (1972). *Mathematical thought from ancient to modern times* (Vol. 1). New York: Oxford University Press.

Kohl, H. (1967). *36 children.* New York: Plume Books.

Kohl, H. (1984). *Growing minds.* New York: Harper & Row.

Lakatos, I. (1976). *Proofs and refutations.* Cambridge: Cambridge University Press.

Lampert, M. (1986). How do teachers manage to teach? *Harvard Educational Review, 55*(2), 178–194.

Lampert, M. (1987). Knowing, doing, and teaching multiplication. *Cognition and Instruction, 3,* 305–342.

Lampert, M. (1989). Choosing and using mathematical tools in classroom discourse. In J. Brophy (Ed.), *Advances in research on teaching* (Vol. 1, pp. 223–264). Greenwich, CT: JAI Press.

Lampert, M. (1990). When the problem is not the question and the solution is not the answer: Mathematical knowing and teaching. *American Educational Research Journal,* 27(1), 29–63.

Lampert, M. (1991). Looking at restructuring within a restructured role. *Phi Delta Kappan,* 72(9), 670–674.

Lampert, M., & Ball, D. L. (1998). *Teaching, multimedia, and mathematics: Investigations of real practice.* New York: Teachers College Press.

Leinhardt, G., Zaslavsky, O., & Stein, M. (1990). Functions, graphs, and graphing: Tasks, learning, and teaching. *Review of Educational Research,* 60(1), 1–64.

Lensmire, T. (1994). *When children write: Cricial re-visions of the writing workshop.* New York: Teachers College Press.

Lortie, D. (1975). *Schoolteacher.* Chicago: University of Chicago Press.

Mack, G. (1970). *Adventures in improvisation at the keyboard.* Evanston, IL: Summy-Birchard.

McLaughlin, M. W., Talbert, J. E., & Bascia, N. (Eds.). (1990). *The contexts of teaching in secondary school: Teachers' realities*. New York: Teachers College Press.

McREL. (1986). *Comprehensive school mathematics program for the intermediate grades*. Aurora, CO: Author.

McREL. (1992). *Comprehensive school mathematics program*. Submission to the Program Effectiveness Panel, U.S. Department of Education. Aurora, CO: Author.

Mehegan, J. (1959). *Jazz improvisation*. New York: Watson-Guptill.

Merrick, G. B. (1987). *Old times on the upper Mississippi*. St. Paul: Minnesota Historical Society.

National Council of Teachers of Mathematics. (1989). *Curriculum and evaluation standards for school mathematics*. Reston, VA: Author.

National Council of Teachers of Mathematics. (1991). *Professional standards for teaching mathematics*. Reston, VA: Author.

National Council of Teachers of Mathematics. (1995). *Assessment standards for school mathematics*. Reston, VA: Author.

National Research Council. (1990). *Reshaping school mathematics*. Washington, DC: National Academy Press.

Novack, C. (1990). *Sharing the dance*. Madison: University of Wisconsin Press.

Paley, V. (1979). *White teacher*. Cambridge, MA: Harvard University Press.

Paley, V. (1981). *Wally's stories*. Cambridge, MA: Harvard University Press.

Paley, V. (1990). *The boy who would be a helicopter*. Cambridge, MA: Harvard University Press.

Peterson, P. (1990). Doing more in the same amount of time: Cathy Swift. *Educational Evaluation and Policy Analysis*, *12*(3), 261–280.

Post, T. R., Behr, M. J., & Lesh, R. (1988). *A potpourri from the rational number project*. Madison: University of Wisconsin, National Center for Research in Mathematical Sciences Education.

Powell, A. G., Farrar, E., & Cohen, D. K. (1985). *The shopping mall high school: Winners and losers in the educational marketplace*. Boston: Houghton Mifflin.

Prawat, R. S. (1992). Are changes in views about mathematics teaching sufficient? The case of a fifth-grade teacher. *Elementary School Journal, 93(2),* 195–211.

Prawat, R. S., & Floden, R. E. (1994). Philosophical perspectives on constructivist views of learning. *Educational Psychologist*, *29*(1), 37–48.

Prawat, R. S., Remillard, J., Putnam, R. T., & Heaton, R. M. (1992). Teaching mathematics for understanding: Case studies of four fifth-grade teachers. *Elementary School Journal*, *93*, 145–152.

Putnam, R. T. (1992). Teaching the "hows" of mathematics for everyday life: A case study of a fifth-grade teacher. *Elementary School Journal, 93(2),* 163–177.

Putnam, R. T., Heaton, R. M., Prawat, R. S., & Remillard, J. (1992). Teaching mathematics for understanding: Discussing case studies of four fifth-grade teachers. *Elementary School Journal*, *93*(2), 213–228.

Reineke, J. W. (1993). *Making connections: Talking and learning in a fourth-grade class.* East Lansing: Michigan State University, Center for the Learning and Teaching of Elementary Subjects.

Remillard, J. (1992). Teaching mathematics for understanding: A fifth-grade teacher's interpretation of policy. *Elementary School Journal, 93(2)*, 179–193.

Remillard, J. (1996). *Changing texts, teachers, and teaching: The role of textbooks in reforms in mathematics education.* Unpublished doctoral dissertation, Michigan State University, East Lansing.

Sarason, S. B. (1982). *The culture of the school and the problem of change.* Boston: Allyn & Bacon.

Schifter, D. (1996). *What's happening in math class?* (Vols. 1–2). New York: Teachers College Press.

Schifter, D., & Fosnot, C. T. (1993). *Reconstructing mathematics education.* New York: Teachers College Press.

Schmidt, W. H. (1996). *Characterizing pedagogical flow: An investigation of mathematics and science teaching in six countries.* Boston: Kluwer Academic.

Schoenfeld, A. H. (1988). Ideas in the air: Speculations on small group learning, environmental and cultural influences on cognition, and epistemology. *International Journal of Educational Research, 13*(1), 71–88.

Schoenfeld, A. H. (1994). Reflections on doing and teaching mathematics. In A. H. Schoenfeld (Ed.), *Mathematical thinking and problem solving* (pp. 53–70). Hillsdale, NJ: Erlbaum.

Scott, J. F. (1969). *A history of mathematics.* New York: Barnes & Noble.

Sedlak, M. W., Wheeler, C. W., Pullin, D. C., & Cusick, P. A. (1986). *Selling students short: Classroom bargains and academic reform in the American high school.* New York: Teachers College Press.

Shulman, L. S. (1986). Those who understand: Knowledge growth in teaching. *Educational Researcher, 15*(2), 4–14.

Shulman, L. S. (1987). Knowledge and teaching: Foundations of the new reform. *Harvard Educational Review, 57*(1), 1–22.

Simon, M. A. (1995). Reconstructing mathematics pedagogy from a constructivist perspective. *Journal for Research in Mathematics Education,* 26(2), 114–145.

Smith, D. E. (1958). *History of mathematics* (Vol. 2). New York: Dover.

Smith, E., & Confrey, J. (1994). Multiplicative structures and the development of logarithms: What was lost by the invention of the function. In G. Harel & J. Confrey (Eds.), *The development of multiplicative reasoning in the learning of mathematics* (pp. 333–360). Albany: State University of New York Press.

Sprague-Mitchell, L. (1963). *Young geographers.* New York: Basic Books.

Steen, L. A. (1990). Pattern. In L. A. Steen (Ed.), *On the shoulders of giants, new approaches to numeracy* (pp. 1–10). Washington, DC: National Academy Press.

Steffe, L. P., & D'Ambrosio, B. S. (1995). Toward a working model of constructivist teaching: A reaction to Simon. *Journal for Research in Mathematics Education*, *26*(2), 146–159.

Stodolsky, S. S. (1988). *The subject matters*. Chicago: University of Chicago Press.

Stuart, J. (1949). *The thread that runs so true*. New York: Scribner's.

Sudnow, D. (1978). *Ways of the hand*. Cambridge, MA: Harvard University Press.

Swafford, J. O., Jones, G. A., & Thornton, C. A. (1997). Increased knowledge in geometry and instructional practice. *Journal for Research in Mathematics Education*, *28*(4), 467–483.

Tall, D. (1992). The transition to advanced mathematical thinking: Functions, limits, infinity and proof. In D. A. Grouws (Ed.), *Handbook for research on mathematics teaching and learning* (pp. 495–511). New York: Macmillan.

Twain, M. (1990). *Life on the Mississippi*. New York: Oxford University Press. (Original work published 1883)

Vergnaud, G. (1988). Multiplicative structures. In J. Hiebert & M. Behr (Eds.), National Council of Teachers of Mathematics, *Number concepts and operations in the middle grades* (pp. 141–161). Hillsdale, NJ: Erlbaum.

Wiemers, N. J. (1990). Transformation and accommodation: A case study of Joe Scott. *Educational Evaluation and Policy Analysis*, *12*(3), 281–292.

Wiggington, E. (1986). *Sometimes a shining moment*. New York: Anchor.

Wilson, S. M. (1990). A conflict of interests: The case of Mark Black. *Educational Evaluation and Policy Analysis*, *12*(3), 293–310.

Yackel, E., & Cobb, P. (1996). Sociomathematical norms, argumentation, and autonomy in mathematics. *Journal for Research in Mathematics Education*, *27*(4), 458–477.

Yackel, E., Cobb, P., & Wood, T. (1991). Small-group interactions as a source of learning opportunities in second-grade mathematics. *Journal for Research in Mathematics Education*, *22*(5), 390–408.

Yinger, R. (1988). The conversation of practice. In P. P. Grimmet & G. L. Erickson (Eds.), *Reflection in teacher education* (pp. 73–94). New York: Teachers College Press.

Index

About the Author

Ruth Heaton received her doctorate in curriculum, teaching, and educational policy from Michigan State University in 1994. Currently Assistant Professor in the Center for Curriculum and Instruction, University of Nebraska–Lincoln, Heaton continues to draw on her teaching experiences and what she learned from them in her work in teacher education and new studies of teacher learning.